WATER
in NORTH

Ivan E Broadhead

MERIDIAN BOOKS

Published 1990 by Meridian Books
© Ivan E Broadhead 1990

British Library Cataloguing in Publication Data
Broadhead, Ivan E
   Waterside Walks in North Yorkshire
   1. North Yorkshire. Recreations: Walking
   I. Title
   796.51094284

   ISBN 1-86992-207-7

Publishers' Note
Every care has been taken in the preparation of this book but the
publishers cannot accept responsibilty for any inaccuracies or for any
loss, damage or inconvenience resulting from the use of the book.

The maps in this book are based upon Ordnance Survey maps, with
the permission of the Controller of Her Majesty's Stationery Office.
© Crown Copyright.

Meridian Books
40 Hadzor Road
Oldbury
Warley
West Midlands
B68 9LA

Maps by Angela Saunders
Printed in Great Britain by BPCC Wheatons Ltd, Exeter.

Contents

Using this book.

Each walk in this book is accompanied by a detailed sketch map which will normally be adequate to enable you to follow the route. However, it is always wise, when you go walking in the country, to have an Ordnance Survey map with you, either from the Landranger series (scale 1:50,000) or, better still, from the more detailed Pathfinder series (Scale 1:25,000). The areas of the Yorkshires Dales and the North Yorkshire Moors are also covered by Outdoor Leisure maps (1:25,000). As well as providing more information on your surroundings, maps are invaluable if, for any reason, you need to curtail your walk, if you get lost or, more likely, if you wish to extend your walk.

Always have a compass, good footwear, adequate waterproofs and, at least on the longer walks, some food and a basic first aid kit.

We have made every effort to ensure that the descriptions of the walks and the accompanying sketch maps are accurate but this cannot be guaranteed. Also, please remember that things do change. Footpaths are sometimes diverted or become overgrown. They may be ploughed over and not reinstated by the farmer (as the law requires). Footbridges may be swept away in floods; coastal paths may be affected by erosion. We hope that you will not encounter any such problems but, if you do, the publishers will be very pleased to hear from you.

Introduction

With the exception of the river Thames probably no waterway has played a more important role in the history of Britain than the Yorkshire Ouse on whose banks was established the City of York. Indeed, water looms large in the annals of North Yorkshire for it has been responsible for contouring the landscape, irrigating its meadows, washing its shores, nurturing a rich harvest of fish, medicating its people, petrifying its products, beautifying its gardens, and providing a water highway for its manufactures.

As if in self-congratulation every river, stream and beck seems to chortle melodiously as it bounces over pebble, rock and sand on its journey to the sea, to be swallowed into that greater mass which roars its majesty by breaking over beach and rocks.

From this rich diversity there have evolved distinctive settlements that owe much of their development to the special nature of their waters. Such places are the spa towns of Harrogate and Scarborough. The famous petrifying well at Knaresborough, draining into the River Nidd, is justly famous, and the little streams running through Thornton-le-Dale have undoubtedly helped it win awards for outstanding beauty. The spectacle of the impressive waterfalls eating away the limestone at Ingleton, and at the opposite side of the county at Goathland, demonstrate the power of water to contour the landscape. The placid waters of gardens at Fountains Abbey make a stark contrast with the foaming waves of the North Sea at Staithes from which fishermen venture forth to harvest Neptune's bounty. And what could be more emotive than the bridge at Glaisdale over the waters which were to have such a profound effect on a love-sick young man?

The walks that follow, then, are intended to enable you, dear reader, to savour some of the variety and contrast that water contributes to North Yorkshire. As Milton put it:

> Meadows trim with daisies pied
> Shallow brooks and rivers wide.
> Towers, and battlements, it sees
> Bosomed high in tufted trees.
> Where perhaps some beauty lies,
> The cynosure of neighbouring eyes.

Ivan E Broadhead
York, 1990

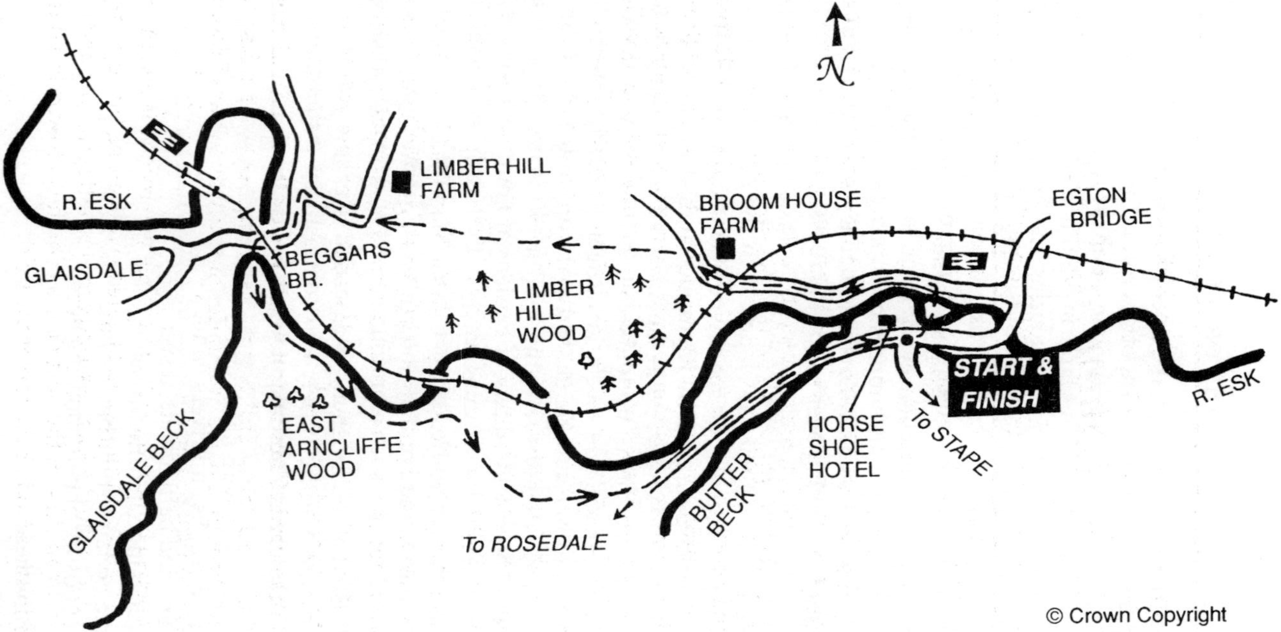

N

EGTON BRIDGE

R. ESK

START & FINISH

To STAPE

HORSE SHOE HOTEL

BUTTER BECK

BROOM HOUSE FARM

LIMBER HILL WOOD

To ROSEDALE

LIMBER HILL FARM

BEGGARS BR.

EAST ARNCLIFFE WOOD

R. ESK

GLAISDALE

GLAISDALE BECK

© Crown Copyright

Labour of Love

GLAISDALE VALLEY

Approx. 3 miles

GLAISDALE is the name of a valley bisected by the River Esk and shut off from the world by the moors, yet it has provided the inspiration for generations of artists and thousands of pictures. And it is also the setting for a truly romantic tale.

Situated about nine miles west of Whitby, in the triangle formed by the A169 Whitby-Pickering and A171 Whitby-Guisborough roads, is Egton Bridge near Grosmont which offers convenient parking space and is where our walk starts. This hamlet, in the wooded valley with its stone bridge over the River Esk, has an imposing Roman Catholic church whose most striking feature is an enormous ribbed roof like the inside of a ship, painted blue and dotted with golden stars. But it is most famous for its Annual Gooseberry Show held on the second Tuesday in August.

Near the *Horse Shoe Hotel*, opposite the Stape road end, is a signpost pointing the way to a public footpath leading to stepping stones which you should follow. Cross the solid stepping stones to an island and a further series of stones to reach the opposite bank where you climb some steps to reach the road.

Turn left towards Glaisdale and walk beside the river which is at first fairly wide and fairly still before becoming rocky and fast flowing. Continue through a wood and under the railway to pass Broom House Farm as you proceed uphill.

After about a hundred yards, and when you reach the end of the wood on the left, go left through a field gate to walk along the top edge of the wood. Follow the track across a stream at a cattle crossing and continue through the middle of the next field as you head towards a dark patch of trees in the wood at the top of the field.

Go through the wood to the right hand side of a hedge bordering a ploughed field and keeping close to the hedge cross a stile at the far corner. From here you can see Egton on the windswept hillside some 550 feet above sea level. The alms-box in its church was made from timber taken from Nelson's flagship, the Victory. Below is Eskdale which attracts students of folklore and searchers of manners and customs of yesteryear.

Having walked across the field and through the yard of Limber Hill Farm, before turning left on the road peep over the hedge at the view of Eskdale winding away to your right. To your left is the valley of Glaisdale and straight ahead the village to which it gives its name. Evidence that it was once an important ironstone mining centre—there were three blast furnaces here in the mid-nineteenth century — is recalled by the neat rows of cottages.

Beggar's Bridge over the River Esk, Glaisdale

Descend on the road and turn left at the road fork before reaching the river with its overhanging trees. A modern road bridge and a railway bridge spanning the river tend to detract a little from the sylvan setting, but a magnet for the artist, photographer, curious, or just plain sentimental is the tiny Beggar's Bridge with its unusually low parapets and a stone with the initials of Thomas Ferris who is said to have built it about 1620.

Legend has it that when young Tom was a young man he had to wade or swim across the river every time he went courting Agnes Richardson, the local squire's daughter. Came the day when he asked for her hand in marriage and the squire told him he was far too poor, indeed beggarly. Tom vowed to make his fortune, marry his sweetheart — and build a bridge so that any who followed in his steps could do so dry-shod. Off he went to Whitby and joined a ship which sailed against the Spanish Armada. He distinguished himself as a sailor, gained much plunder and returned to carry out his vow — this time the squire gave his consent. Tom took his bride to Hull where he became both richer and mayor before dying in 1631. His tale was immortalised in verse:

> The rover came back from a far distant land,
> And claimed from the maiden her long-promised hand;
> But he built, ere he won her, the bridge of his vow,
> And the lovers of Egton pass over it now.

On the other side of the railway is a footbridge over Glaisdale Beck which you cross to climb up the bank to enter East Arncliff Wood sometimes called Egton Wood. Then turn left on a narrow path which begins by following the line of the river. Known as the Packman's Trod the path is partially paved through the woods and initially it is about a hundred feet above the river, but when it drops down to water level it can sometimes be muddy. Sight and sound of the river are lost as the path climbs once again until, at a clearing, there is a birds-eye view of a fine fall below.

After passing a rocky outcrop on the right and a pond the woodlands thin out to reveal high cliffs on the right. Once again the sound of rushing water draws attention to a stretch of white water below before you reach the Egton Bridge to Rosedale road which will return you to your starting point.

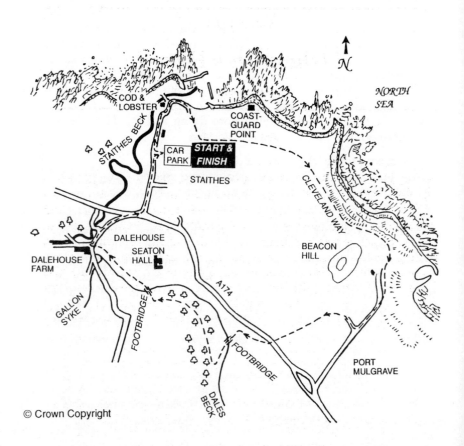

© Crown Copyright

Fishermen's Friend

STAITHES

Approx. 3½ Miles

PERHAPS THE LEAST CHANGED FISHING VILLAGE on the Yorkshire Coast is Staithes about ten miles north of Whitby on the A174. In its heyday the village boasted some 120 boats, and 300 men were employed in the fishing trade. In addition, the women played an active role, assisting with the drying and repairing of nets, baiting hooks, launching boats, gutting fish and knitting the heavy woollens which their menfolk needed. From 1885 a railway link also gave a boost to trade with three trains a week taking the fish to inland cities. The advent of steam trawlers from larger ports killed the livelihood but in recent years salmon and lobster fishing has created a

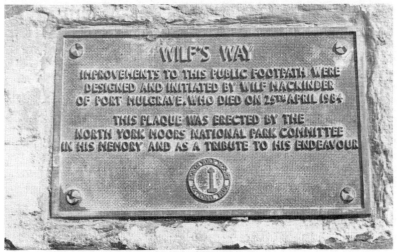

Plaque on clifftop marker

resurgence of interest in the seafaring tradition to make Staithes the tenth largest lobster port in England and Wales.

Starting from the village car park the walk begins with a right hand turn downhill into the old village and along to the *Cod and Lobster* where you turn right up the road. With the harbour behind continue uphill and bear left up a gulley to pass to the left of some farm buildings. The cottage where Captain James Cook was born in 1728 has long since gone as has the shop generally spoken of as a "hucksters" where he was apprenticed as a boy, but unfortunately an unpleasant story of his having taken a shilling from his master's till, when the attractions of the sea proved too much for him to resist, persistently clings to all accounts of his early life here.

The path now swings uphill to the cliff edge with some dramatic views because just a couple of miles north of the village at Boulby, some 666 feet above sea level, are the highest cliffs on the east coast and, with one

Royal Jet

Jet from the cliffs hereabouts once shone like a black jewel in the best Royal court circles in Europe, and created a thriving industry in nearby Whitby. In 1864 the income from jet was worth £90.000 and some of the products are preserved in the Whitby Museum.

Jet, a form of coal that can be polished until it gleams, can be found running in horizontal seams inland from the cliffs where the 'jet holes' of the miners can still be seen. Jet has been found in ancient barrows, and the Romans used it to carve ornaments. Craftsmen in Whitby have always worked it but it was not until about 1820 that men began to be regularly employed. Thirty years later, several firms were established including Thomas Andrews, jet ornament makers to Her Majesty Queen Victoria, whose fondness for the black jewellery, particularly after the death of Prince Albert, did much to boost the Whitby industry. The fashion caught on in France and large quantities of necklaces, bracelets, rings, brooches and ornaments for hats and bonnets were exported. The Queen of Bavaria ordered a jet cable-chain guard nearly five feet long. At its peak around 1870 jet employed 1,400 men and boys in Whitby but a change in fashion, Spanish imports and the use of inferior jet and imitations led to a swift decline and by 1936 only five men were working jet. Today there appears to be only one carrying on the tradition.

exception, on the entire coastline of England. Soon you reach the road which you should join to enter Port Mulgrave, once an important link in the mining industry hereabouts. From 1875 to 1934 ironstone was worked at Grinkle mines and transported by rope hauled wagons to Port Mulgrave for shipment by sea. Near the site of the early mining activity now stands a potash mine, the only one of its kind in the country, but the product is not shipped through Port Mulgrave.

Opposite the telephone box turn right past some buildings and at the last one turn sharp left to cross the fields and follow the path downhill to the A174 main road. Cross this into the layby and go left over a stile as the path leads you downhill into a pleasant wooded valley. After

Looking down on Port Mulgrave

crossing a footbridge over Dales Beck bear left up the path before swinging sharply back and leaving the woodland to cross open scrubland. As you continue downhill you pass a caravan site on your right before turning right to cross a bridge over Dales Beck to join a track which leads you to a road at Dalehouse. Turn right and follow the road uphill to once again meet the A174 and bear right a short distance before going left into Staithes and back to the car park.

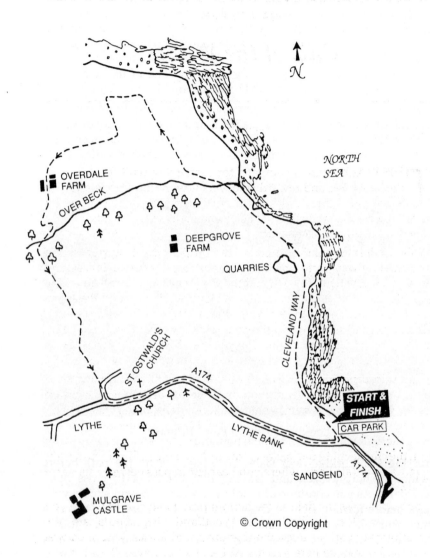

© Crown Copyright

Call of the Waves

SANDSEND

Approx. 3 miles

THIS WALK takes as company for part of its circuit the waters of the North Sea and rewards the walker with fine seascape views. Sandsend is three miles north of Whitby and easily reached by the A174 coast road which, at the north end of the village, leads directly and conveniently into a car park.

Walk up the steps at the far end of the car park and turn right along the former railway route which hugs the cliff tops. If the sun is breaking through a heavy tent of clouds and the sky is chasing grey all down the heavens, then the sea below changes colour every moment. What has been brown and sullen reflects the softest tints of green, while beyond it is all grey and silver. A rough sea, tossing into sparkles, brushed by myriads of sea-birds and glancing up the rocks in vivid flashes, is driven along the sands of the bay in a singular translucent mist.

After skirting some quarries turn right up the bank by the entrance to the old railway tunnel. At the top of the steps turn right for about a dozen paces before crossing a stile and following a path across a field, keeping the fence on the left. At the far end cross the stile and bear left along the cliff path. At the next field boundary turn left once again away from the cliff keeping the hedge on the right. At the field gate turn right towards Overdale Farm where you bear left to pass between the farm buildings.

Continue across the field to the bottom right hand corner where you enter a wood by a bridlegate. Woodlands hereabouts are the repositories of curious tales about gnomes and fairies. One such was Jeannie; she may be here still for all I know but few will go looking when they hear what befell a suitor some years ago. He was a local farmer and he rode up on horseback calling her name. Whether he omitted any title of respect or whether it was merely the unwelcome attention which enraged the irritable Jeannie, I do not know. But she

tried to strike the unlucky farmer with her wand as she chased him away
so fast that even the fleetness of the horse failed to help him escape. He
galloped to a beck which he leapt in the very nick of time. But Jeannie was
upon him and, as the horse leaped forward, her wand fell on his back
cutting him in two so that Jeannie kept his hind quarters on her side of the
water while the farmer with head and forelegs fell on the safe side of the
flowing stream — which fairies cannot cross!

Clifftop walk at Sandsend

You go over the beck and follow the path upwards through the wood to
reach a hedged track towards Lythe Church. Keeping the hedge on the left
as you proceed forward over a stile you will eventually reach the A174 at
Lythe with the village to your right and the church of St Oswald on your
left. You are here 450 feet above the North Sea with nothing to hinder the
view of cornfields sloping down the high cliffs, ships passing for ever along
the coast, and the distant vista of Whitby Abbey overlooking the harbour.
One of the rectors here from 1307/15 — William de Melton — later held
office as Archbishop of York for twenty three years whilst John Fisher who
served as rector from 1499 to 1504 became a Cardinal but was executed for
treason in 1535 at the Tower of London. The church registers and accounts
include some curious entries including in 1707 a payment of four shillings
and a penny for "Ringers wages on the Rejoicing Day for the Union
between England and Scotland" and in 1829 four shillings and fivepence
was spent on "candles, tobacco and pipes."

Proceed down Lythe Bank with its breathtaking views over the golden
sands towards Whitby and keep an extra careful look-out for traffic at the
bottom of the hill as you return to the car park from which you started.

Sweet Secret of the Spout

GOATHLAND

Approx. 2 miles

GOATHLAND — about eight miles south of Whitby and well signposted from the A169 — is the starting point for this walk which begins on the opposite side of the green from the Parish Church and on the right hand side (as you face the building) of the *Mallyan Spout Hotel* adjacent to which is ample parking space. It is signposted and well trodden. The path plunges down a steep hillside and, towards the bottom, enters a plantation of perfumed conifers. Down below you will find a signpost. The right turn is for Beck Hole; the left turn leads up the rocky course of the stream to the fall.

Brave the rocks and see Mallyan Spout — one of the sweet secrets of the North Yorkshire Moors which hides away in this deep valley amply shrouded by trees. The water tumbles in

Mallyan Spout, Goathland

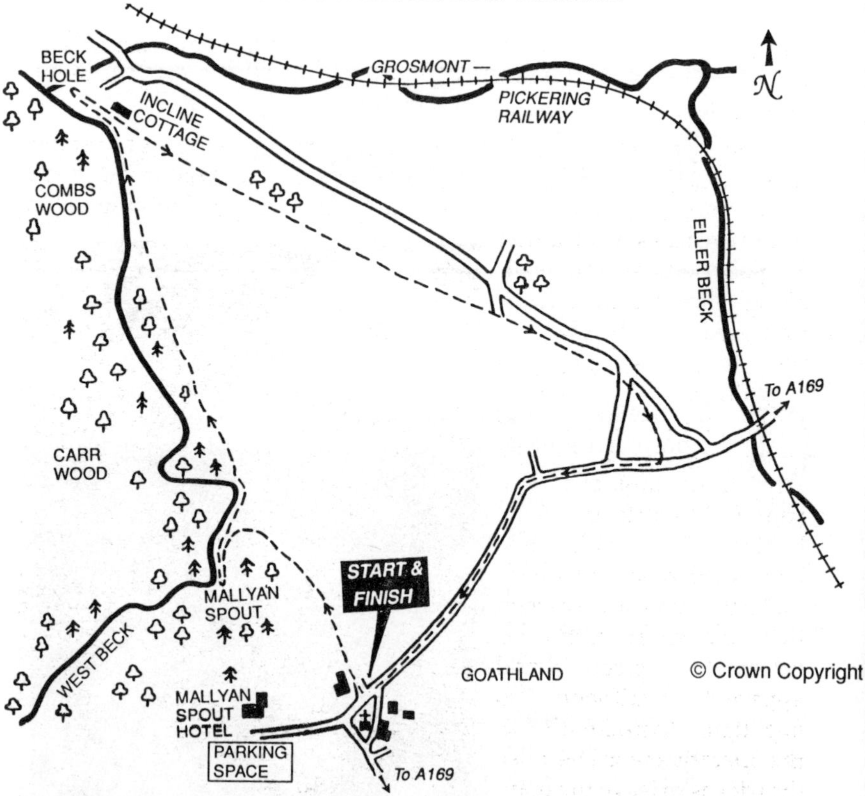

BECK HOLE

GROSMONT —

PICKERING RAILWAY

INCLINE COTTAGE

COMBS WOOD

ELLER BECK

To A169

CARR WOOD

MALLYAN SPOUT

START & FINISH

WEST BECK

GOATHLAND

© Crown Copyright

MALLYAN SPOUT HOTEL

PARKING SPACE

To A169

Village Green, Goathland

a fine spray down a face of green rocks and it would be possible to take a shower under Mallyan because the foot of the fall is reasonably accessible.

Having braved the rocks to see Mallyan, return to the signpost and take the path to Beck Hole. Again it is a good path, well trodden and easy to follow. The route climbs rapidly and steeply from the valley until it reaches a meadow. To your left, as you walk along, the stream can be glimpsed far below. To your right is spread a magnificent panorama, with the village of Goathland in the foreground and a superb rim of moorland rising behind. The path then begins the descent to Beck Hole but you are warned that one short section is extremely steep and apparently difficult to negotiate. "Apparently" is the operative word because the trick is to leave the main path at the brink of the precipice and find an easier way down through the

Beck Hole

woodland to the right. This can be accomplished without undue hardship and without venturing far from the path.

Continue along the path at the bottom and you will arrive at a gate beyond which is a broad swathe of well-cropped grass and a pleasant stone building called Incline Cottage. This is a relic of the old horse railway opened between Whitby and Pickering in 1836.

Go through the gate, turn left and join the track which leads past a small bungalow on the right and to another gate beyond. Go through this gate and in a short time you will find yourself in Beck Hole.

The climb back to your starting point can be accomplished by going back as far as the line of the old railway and following the track past Incline Cottage and up the incline to Goathland.

Where Something Stirs

LANGDALE FOREST

Approx. 3½ miles — hard going, severe in patches.

FROM THE A170 PICKERING/SCARBOROUGH ROAD turn north at Snainton signposted to Troutsdale. After driving through seven miles of superb wooded scenery turn left to Broxa and half a mile further on bear left to the car park at Langdale Bridge where our walk starts. From here, go through a wooden gate and take the footpath which leads North alongside the River Derwent.

Walk into the silent forest with its huge ant-hills, abundant rabbits, but comparatively few birds. A great forest was once a great temptation. Nowadays few people resort to poaching, but a picture of how bad the old days were can be found in the *Coucher Book of Pickering*. It is recorded here that the Rector of Middleton was desperately fond of coursing and kept four greyhounds for that purpose. Allan, huntsman of the Abbot of Whitby, together with Thomas Newall and some other wicked persons took a hind using the Abbot's dogs and the venison went to the Abbey. This was on 8 March 1294. There is a deadly precision about the date which forbids any doubt about the scandal. They were all outlawed as were Robert Acklam, Geoffrey Lepington, John Dukes and George Acklam, with a few more who made up a pleasant hunting party about the same time. Somebody must have been watching them all day for it is recorded that they took three hinds with bows and arrows as well as other game. Soon they had nothing to do but hunt, for they followed Allan into outlawry and the vast green woods where you now tread.

After walking along the riverside for about 1½ miles cross the wooden bridge before turning left along the bank and almost immediately, at the symbol of a hiker, turn right into the dense gloom of the mature forest. This is followed by a nose-scraping climb with helpful log risers in the hillside. You may enjoy the feeling of pioneering darkest Langdale with waymarkings giving a sense of security. Turn right at

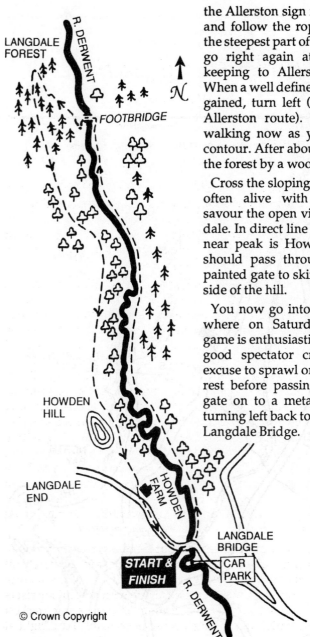

the Allerston sign nailed to a tree and follow the rope handrail up the steepest part of the climb; then go right again at the top still keeping to Allerston markings. When a well defined forest road is gained, turn left (discarding the Allerston route). There is level walking now as you follow the contour. After about ¾ mile leave the forest by a wooden gate.

Cross the sloping field (which is often alive with rabbits) and savour the open views across the dale. In direct line of the path the near peak is Howden Hill; you should pass through the white painted gate to skirt the left hand side of the hill.

You now go into a cricket field where on Saturdays a village game is enthusiastically fought — good spectator cricket and an excuse to sprawl on the grass and rest before passing through the gate on to a metalled road and turning left back to the car park at Langdale Bridge.

© Crown Copyright

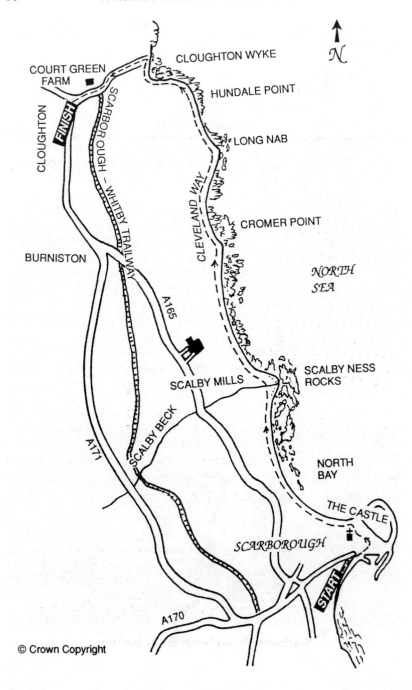

© Crown Copyright

Fair Start from the Spa

SCARBOROUGH

Approx. 6 miles. Return by bus or walk along the old railway (about 5 miles).

START AT THE GRAND HOTEL, completed in 1867 by Cuthbert Brodrick the architect of Leeds Town Hall, which guards the cliff top overlooking the South Bay. A plaque marks the site of the house where Anne Brontë died in 1849. Turn right along St Nicholas Street with the Town Hall dating from 1852 and Bell Mansion(1708) on the right. On the left is the *Royal Hotel* (1862-1870-1935) which incorporates the eighteenth century "Long Room" and has a fine staircase. Also on the left is the former Town Hall(1870) now Lloyds Bank.

Turn right at the cross roads to go along Newborough and right again to the Market Hall(1853) which you go through into Saint Sepulchre

Scarborough Castle across the harbour

Street which has some pleasant eighteenth century houses. On the right is the former St John's Church (1884) and the Trinity House almshouses (1832). On the left is the former Friend's meeting House (1801). At the end, in Princess Square, the *Leeds Hotel* (1693, restored 1900) and opposite what remains of the medieval Butter Cross allied with the famous song of *Scarborough Fair*.

Butter Cross and St Mary's Church, Scarborough

Go straight along Princess Street, probably the best and least altered of Old Town streets, and turn left up Castlegate. Go left again along Long Westgate and at the corner of St Mary's Street is a house built in 1688. Here turn right up St Mary's Stairs into St Mary's Churchyard. In the churchyard extension is the grave of Anne Brontë. Adjacent is a short street named Paradise in which is a plaque claiming it as the reputed birthplace in 1773 of Sir George Cayley, pioneer of aerodynamics. The church dates from the twelfth century and the East end ruins were caused by gunfire from the Castle during the Civil War siege.

Cross the churchyard into Castle Road and turn right and then left through Mulgrave Place, where there are some sham crenellated castles on the right, to the top of North Cliff. There is a panoramic view of North Bay here. Turn right up the steps and along the path to the Castle. The remains of a Roman Signal Station AD370 and the Castle, with its magnificent Keep begun late

The Birth of Tourism?

As 'Queen of the Coast', Scarborough lays claim to being the place were the English tourist industry began, but there were visitors long before that. Skarthi, a Viking chief built a wooden fortified settlement here. In 1066, a warlike Harald Hardrada burnt it down by hurling flaming brands from Castle Hill. Later, William le Gross built a castle, and Henry II improved on it and created a massive fortress, around which the town began to grow. The catalyst to the tourist business came in 1626 when a local woman, Mrs Ann Farrow, found soothing relief from her rheumaticky aches and pains from a mineral spring spouting out of the cliffs at South Bay. From this crystal spring developed Scarborough Spa. Soon the corporation was bottling the water and making £70 a year, a fortune in those days, by selling it to visitors. It even brought in a bye-law — fining folk sixpence on each half gallon if they took it away in casks and vessels without permission from a minister or churchwarden.

An important, but unwelcome, visitor in 1646 was Oliver Cromwell who came to besiege the castle and is commemorated by the Mount named after him on which now sits the town's 75 ft high war memorial.

More profitable visitors were those who visited the "Spaw" run by a well-known eccentric Dickie Dickinson. He sat outside a wooden cottage by the wells with his monkey and dog supervising the supply of waters to tourists. He also had a sideline selling gingerbread and cleaning shoes, and he thoughtfully installed the first public toilets! In 1737 the wells were buried by a landslide but the waters were rediscovered after five weeks.

By the end of the eighteenth century sea bathing was also considered healthy as well as pleasurable, and Scarborough took advantage of the new vogue to consolidate its status as a tourist centre. A rebuilt spa was attracting the rich and fashionable, and with the coming of the railway in 1845 the floodgates opened with a massive influx of visitors. Within forty years the population burgeoned from 13,000 to 33,000 and many fine houses and hotels were built, including the imposing and unique Grand Hotel which has dominated the town since 1876. Despite many setbacks the spa, and its hall in which artists including Sir Henry Irving, George Robey and Lily Langtry once entertained capacity audiences, has continued to develop so ensuring Scarborough's claim to a regal position in popular tourism.

twelfth century and ruined after the Civil War, can be inspected.

Walk along Mulgrave Terrace, Rutland Terrace and Blenheim Terrace to descend Albert Road to Royal Albert Drive and continue forward along the seafront. There is a mixture of beach and rock as you head north towards Scalby Mills where Scalby Beck rushes out to sea. After passing the luxurious homes on the cliff sides at Scalby Mills open fields run off to the horizon on the left as you proceed towards Scalby Ness Rocks. At low water there is a wide vista of exposed rock pools and great slabs of rock washed by the receding tide. Continue past Cromer Point and along the coastal path past the Coast Guard look-out post at Long Nab as it

Anne Brontë's grave, Scarborough

sweeps down from Hundale Point. The high cliffs to Hayburn Wyke and the *Hayburn Wyke Hotel* run off to the right at the tiny cove of Cloughton Wyke where you turn left. The track crosses the old Whitby coastal railway by bridge before you enter a shallow valley.

Climb through the trees past Court Green Farm buildings along a track which brings you into Cloughton village where the main road bends sharply to the right. From here a Skipper bus, running at half-hourly intervals (hourly on Sundays), will return you to Scarborough. However, if you want to extend your walk you can return along the Scarborough and Whitby Trailway which follows the route of the former railway line that linked the two towns.

Access is from Station Lane nearly opposite Cloughton Hall and through the old goods yard where the original warehouse stands. Construction of the twenty mile long Scarborough & Whitby Railway started in June 1872 but by 1877 work was at a standstill due to lack of investment. New engineers and contractor were appointed in 1879 and the railway was completed by July 1855 when it was opened to the public.

Due to steep gradients and sharp curves the average speed of trains was 20 mph, earning it the nickname of the Steep & Winding Railway. However, revenue was not sufficient to warrant its upkeep and the last trains ran on 6 March 1965.

Follow the trailway through Scalby where a small housing estate occupies the site of the former station. Continue forward until you reach Peasholme Beck where it is crossed by Woodland Ravine. Leave the Trailway here and bear left into Manor Road and follow this right until you join Wykeham Street where you turn left. This becomes Roscoe Street and at its junction with Westborough turn left to pass the railway station on your right as you proceed into Newborough from which you turn right down Bar Street to Falconers Road back to the Grand Hotel.

Village Idyll

THORNTON LE DALE

Approx. 2 miles

SPECULATION ABOUNDS about the origin of the name Thornton Dale — or Thornton le Dale as the locals prefer. Before the Norman Conquest the holder of the manor was named Tor and the termination *-ton* clearly indicates an Anglo-Saxon settlement which was either a clearing in a wood or an enclosed farmstead. In its earliest recorded form the name was Torenton and 'Dale' does not appear until the early nineteenth century. No matter, it is regarded by many people as the prettiest village in the county and it boasts many interesting antiquities including a market cross, stocks on the village green which have not been used for over a century — and the imposing church of All Saints which dates from the fourteenth century. Inside is a

The path through Thornton le Dale

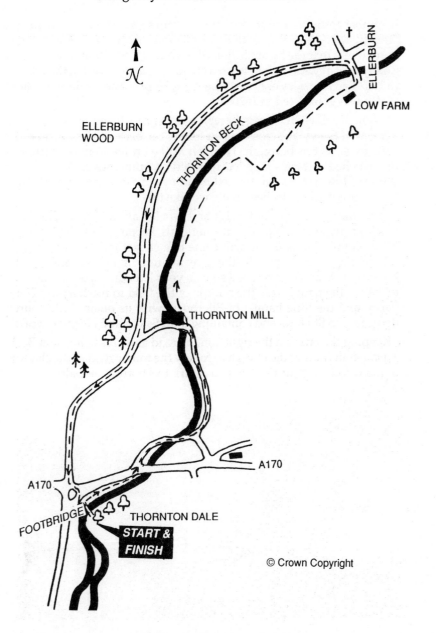

© Crown Copyright

recumbent effigy supposed by some to represent Sir Richard Cholmley, "the great Black Knight of the North" who died in 1578, but it seems more likely that the figure is that of a woman. The Cholmleys lived at Roxby Hall of which slight traces remain half a mile west of the village. In 1657 Lady Lumley endowed the Alms Houses and Grammar School which was completed in 1670.

Behind a screen of trees is a convenient car park and the walk starts in front of the village cross as you follow the beck alongside the A170 road towards Scarborough. Turn left at the bridge to pass in front of the thatched cottage which has featured on numerous calendars. This is one of the many cruck-framed buildings in the village, all of which would originally have been thatched like this.

Cross the beck by the footbridge and turn left along the road until you reach a private car park. Walk through this, keeping the mill (Thornton Mill) on your left and you will come to a step stile. Go over this and follow the path alongside the stream until it bears right up the hedgeside. You will soon see a stile on your left which you should take to follow the path across the middle of the field to reach a farm (Low Farm) and the little hamlet of Ellerburn, with its quaint little church dedicated to St Hilda and containing both Saxon and Norman work.

Keeping the farm on the right join the road and cross Thornton Beck. Turn left in front of the church to follow the minor road in the shadow of the woods to your right as you return to Thornton le Dale.

Some Thornton Characters

Many a tale stems from The Square. Before the Second World War one Charlie Myers used to run a bus service with a 1922 Ford 14-seater from there. On Fridays and Saturdays his destination was Malton, via Yedingham and it was not unusual for a farmer to climb on board with a small pig or lamb under his arm. On Saturday evenings he ran a "picture bus" to Pickering cinema. It was often said that passengers could have walked home quicker than Charlie drove the bus.

Another famous local character was Willie Ecclesfield who worked as hound feeder and kennel man to the squire Richard Hill. On the morning he was to be married he asked the squire if there was anything special he wanted doing, as he could put off the wedding until it was convenient.

Willie used to play the flute in the church band but when an organ was bought he was told he wouldn't be needed. This did not suit Willie and on one or two occasions he burst into tune with the flute during the service. He would take no notice of the rector and was finally banned from the church. Old Willie died in March 1872.

Also buried in the graveyard is Matthew Grimes who was 96 when he died in 1875. He was a grand old soldier who fought in India and in the Peninsular War, his proudest boast being that he stood guard over Naploeon at St Helena and helped carry to his grave the dictator who had shaken Europe to its foundations.

Even shopping in the village was bound up with religion at the turn of the century according to Macdonald Wigfield who recalled a rare youthful 'trespass' during his upbringing here. At that time there were two of almost every kind of shop, one kept by a member of the Church of England and the other by a Methodist, and people shopped accordingly. In 1905 Colman's Mustard celebrated the Trafalgar centenary by issuing with each box a postcard of Napoleon or one of the stirring incidents of his career. To advertise this the firm issued to shops a poster showing the eight cards in the series. In 1906 one was displayed in the window of the Church of England grocer, but young Wigfield was told firmly that the family did not trade there. At length, after a lot of chagrin, his eldest aunt took him to the shop and explained the situation whereupon the shopkeeper presented him with a duplicate poster.

Unlucky Seven

ROSEDALE ABBEY

Approx. 2½ miles

TURN OFF THE A170 SCARBOROUGH/THIRSK ROAD at Wrelton and drive up through grand scenery to Rosedale Abbey where there is ample parking space.

This journey is rewarded by a colourful reflection of the changing seasons. In spring there is the 'greening' of the moors followed, in early summer, by a wonderful variety of wild flowers and blossoms. The glowing purples of heather in August and September are a prelude to the deep red berries of the mountain ash and the russet carpet of dying heather before winter submerges everything, except the dark green forests, under a dazzling white carpet.

Walk across the village green past the school and turn right up the lane past the cottages. In thirty yards turn left at footpath sign and go through a caravan site to reach the River Seven. The path is clearly marked by stiles and gates.

From the river source at Seven Stone to Hartoft End, Rosedale stretches for eight miles, its width varying from about 1¼ miles from Thorgill to Clough House, to less than half a mile at Hartoft End. Compressed into this tiny dale is an amazing variety of scenery ranging from heather moor and bogs made vivid with cotton-grass in mid-summer, to rocky defiles, wooded gorges, and 'holmes' or water meadows.

Continue along the footpath, with the river on your left, for about ¾ mile until you are opposite a white painted bridge with gates at each end. If you are fortunate you will probably see heron flapping up from the water. Fishermen complain that there are no trout here due to peat being flushed downstream after heavy rains — but are the herons just living on voles then?

Over to your right is Bell End Farm. In 1960 a hearth post bearing a

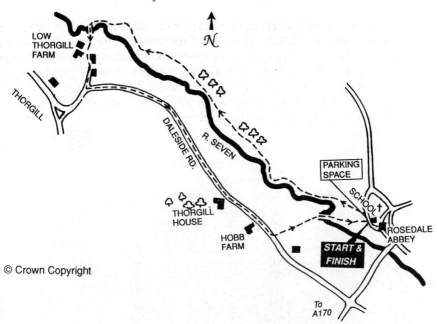

© Crown Copyright

'witch mark' was removed from here to Ryedale Folk Museum —
superstition lingered long in the Dales. One of the most famous
Rosedale witches was Hester Wood who, so it was said, could use her
evil eye with dire result and was able, when she wished, to turn herself
into a cat!

Cross the bridge, and continue along the path past two caravans and
out through the metal gate into the farmyard of Low Thorgill Farm.
Turn left up the farm track to the road and left again along Daleside
Road.

Rosedale hilltops are pocked with quarry dumps and the story of
ironstone mining is told on the National Park notice board in the
village. Some say jet was also got hereabouts and fashioned into
jewellery at Whitby.

This industrial activity has resulted in a number of derelict and ruined
houses which date from the nineteenth century when the dale became
a little 'Klondyke'. Some indication of the rapid change caused by the
development of ironstone mining is the population growth from 548 in
1851 to 2,839 twenty years later in the heyday of the mining boom. By
1901 it had declined to 1,396, and by 1961 the figure was 286.

Earlier, in the late sixteenth century, French glassworkers from the

Kentish Weald began operations in Rosedale which was chosen for its supply of oak timber, siliceous sand, bracken (for potash and lime) and plentiful amounts of clay. Local freestone was used to build a 25 ft long by 18 ft wide furnace (preserved since 1970 in Ryedale Folk Museum at Hutton-le-Hole) with two crucible holders to make vessel glass. Excellent quality goblets, flasks, tumblers, bottles and linen smoothers were all produced in green 'forest glass'.

Continue along Daleside Road past Thorgill House and Hobb Farm, then, opposite the caravan site, take the public footpath diagonally across the field to Rosedale Abbey. On reaching the street directly facing and set in a small field is a stone column; the Nun's Staircase.

These spiralling steps are all that is left of Rosedale Priory, a Cistercian Nunnery founded about 1158 and dissolved in 1535. Thereafter the warm coloured stone was carted away to build neighbouring houses,

A "Witch Mark" in Ryedale Folk Museum

Symbols like this, carved on the supporting posts of cottage hearths, were said to deter witches

farms, walls. Vandalism or re-cycling? Perhaps it depends whether you look at it with twentieth century eyes or from the point of view of sixteenth century needs. Indeed, some of the previous inhabitants seem to have been of dubious reputation. In the days before all the timber had been cut down all the tenants of the district were subject to forest laws. In a charter of 1223, when various wooded areas were bequeathed, Rosedale is described as a 'nest of poachers'. Inhabitants of the dale were frequently hauled up before the courts in Pickering for offences of this nature; also for taking 'green' wood or 'assarting' (enclosing) land — even the Prioress was summonsed for this!

ROSEDALE PRIORY

A relic of a better age, debased
And turned to worldly use, where gold and greed
Strive in the place of prayer; and yet
The hallowed stones their sacred mission tell,
Nor suffer gain to still the voice of praise.

That was how one old anonymous poet saw the ruins of the priory that Robert, son of Nicholas de Stuteville founded about 1190. Like the sister priory at Keldholme, it was under the protection and patronage of the highest Yorkshire aristocracy, although it was hidden away in one of the oldest districts. According to the Chancellor's Roll of 1200 William de Stuteville gave one palfrey for confirmation of the nuns of 'Rusendale'; but although the reason for his generosity was obvious he did not make the gift entirely good because in 1201 he is set down as still owing it. This William de Stuteville was the friend and favourite whom King John in that year made Sheriff of Yorkshire, an office for which William paid £1,000 to have so long as he did well and faithfully serve the crown. It did not last long for he died in 1207.

Little is known about the nuns and whether they were Benedictines or Cistercians. One ecclesiastical record describes them as "monales Albae" — white nuns. However a charter from King John on 16 August in the eleventh year of his reign says:

"John, by the grace of God etc., greetings. Know ye that we have conceded, and by this our charter confirmed, to God, to the Blessed Mary and to St Lawrence Rosedale, and to the nuns serving God, the reasonable gift which Robert de Stuteville made to them in free, pure, and perpetual alms, of the Vale of Rosedale with all its appurtenances, different charters of the same Robert; and of the whole meadow of Bagghthwaite as the charter of the said Robert which the aforesaid possess, properly tested; and in like manner all the tan-bark of the wood of the same Robert as far as Cropton; cut under supervision of our forester. Whereof, we wish and firmly enjoin that the aforesaid nuns may have and hold the aforesaid tenements, and all their appurtenances, well and in peace, freely and quietly, wholly and fully, in all places and things, with all liberties and free customs belonging to them as is aforesaid."

But the Scots were not concerned with the "peace and quiet" of Yorkshire priories and on 20 November 1322 Archbishop Melton had to disperse the nuns on account of the damage that the house had received at the hands of marauding Scotsmen.

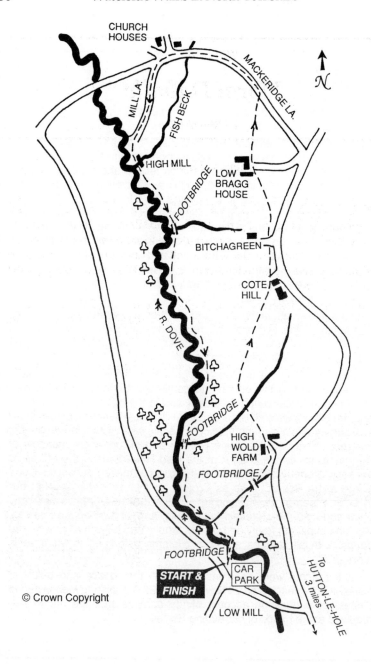

© Crown Copyright

Floral Dawdle

FARNDALE

Approx. 3½ miles

THE DAFFODIL FIELDS OF FARNDALE are one of the finest Spring sights in the North. Wild daffodils grow in profusion in the fields and among the trees alongside the tiny twisting River Dove. How they came to the whole valley is not known, but legend says that they were planted by monks from Rievaulx Abbey in the twelfth and thirteenth centuries.

Five miles from Pickering on the A170 Scarborough/Thirsk road turn at the Farndale signpost for the picturesque village of Hutton-le-Hole. Its houses appear scattered as though by chance around a green common, and its beck is crossed here and there by bridges and fords. I recommend a stop to look around before continuing on to Low Mill

Looking up Farndale

where the walk starts. Apart from the obvious attractions of the village, the Ryedale Folk Museum, which is housed there, is well worth a visit. In various impressive early eighteenth century farm buildings you will find displays concentrating on the origins, crafts and superstitions of Ryedale folk since the Stone Age. Of particular interest is a unique Elizabethan glass furnace recovered from Rosedale which is the destination of Walk Four. The museum is the venue for the national championships of the game of merils, held here every year.

I suggest you then drive up the west side of the vale to the start of your walk and return down the east — in either case there is a feast of open moorland scenery for six miles to Low Mill car park, with heather, ling, and bracken carpeting the high tableland with a purple sea, splashes of green and autumnal browns setting the moors ablaze with colour in the evening sun. Bell heather, tormentil, milk wort, cowberry, and crowberry are just a few plant species which add variety to these uplands.

From the car park walk through the gate down to the bridge over the River Dove — which is connected with the famous ghost story of Sarkless Kitty (see panel — page 34) and then up along the stone causeway. Cross over the white painted bridge before the stile on the path which takes you up to High Wold Farm.

Turn left along the farm track with sheep and pheasants in the fields for company and take the upper gate before following the hedge on the left and going uphill almost to Cote Hill farm. Cross the field to a wooden gate by red roofed piggeries and an old thatched cottage — wheat thatching was formerly commonplace.

Go on to the cart track through Bitchagreen farm yard, cross two fields to Low Bragg House and taking the top gate walk across the field to Mackeridge Lane. Turn left along the lane into Church Houses hamlet. The *Feversham Arms* has a fine cast iron cooking range with adjustable pot hooks, still, after a hundred years, in working order: The range was made at Kirbymoorside and uses half a bag of coal at a fuelling.

Pass down the side of the car park and walk along Mill Lane to High Mill — an old corn mill with the wheel long gone but the wheel chamber and some of the gear still remaining. Here is the confluence of Fish Beck and the River Dove. A delightful path follows a stream that curves and bends its way back to Low Mill. Until thirty years ago the mill was grinding meal for pigs and the miller also operated a saw mill cutting timber for the Feversham estate. Coal and iron was mined on the hilltops and many trades were followed. Up there on the moors stands the great rock-tumulus called Obtrush, home, so it is said, of a goblin — for superstition lingered long hereabouts. Now the Dale is quiet — except for six weeks when the daffodils are in bloom; then it is necessary to impose a one-way traffic system. In 1955 a Local Nature Reserve was established here and under a local bye-law it is now an offence to pick the daffodils so this ensures that the masses of blooms remain for the enjoyment of all.

The Hob of Farndale

The tradition of the 'hob' is strong hereabouts. A hob is an elf or hobgoblin who helps or hinders a farmer according to the farmer's attitude. The most well known is Hob o'Hurst of Farndale.

Ralph, a strong, hard-working lad on a Farndale farm was killed in a blizzard on the moors. Soon afterwards a loud thumping was heard in the middle of the night. The farmer investigated and found inside his barn more corn threshed than one man could have done in a week.

The noises continued every night but the farmer ignored them because every morning he found some work had been done around the farm, speedily and efficiently. It was thought that Ralph had come back as a hob. This free labour enabled the farmer to prosper and in gratitude he left the hob a large jug of cream and bread and butter every night.

His son continued to do the same when his father died and when he died his son inherited the farm and the hob. But this man's wife was thrifty to the point of meanness. She substituted skimmed milk for the cream. The hob was angry. He did no more work and became mischievous and malicious. So unbearable did life become that the farmer and his wife packed their belongings on a cart and set off for a home without a hob. On the way they met a neighbour. "Ah see thoo's flittin" he said.

"Ay, we'se flittin" said a voice from the back of the cart. "Ah'm part o' t' possessions!" There, to the chagrin of the farmer and his wife, sat the hob! They realised they were defeated. They sighed and eyed the hob. "Eh well — if thoo's theer flittin with us, we may as well gan yam ageean!"

Much of the peculiar local dialect is akin to Norse so *flittin* is removing, *gan* is go, and *yam* is home.

The Tale of Sarkless Kitty

In bygone days a 'sark' was a 'vest' or'shift' and to be 'sarkless' meant to be naked. So Sarkless Kitty was a peculiar ghost who did not even sport the traditional shroud.

Apparently Kitty was simply an ordinary young girl who used to live and work as a servant at a farm near to where Lowna Bridge now stands, although at the time there was only a ford across the River Dove. She had become attached to the son of a Gillamoor farmer who lived at the top of the steep hill on the opposite side of the river. His parents were not very happy at the association with a serving girl and so meetings had to be clandestine.

Often he would come on horseback across the ford to meet his sweetheart. One stormy winter's day when the river was in full flood the young lovers had arranged to meet, but apparently the young farmer failed to turn up. Whether Kitty had thrown herself into the stream in a fit of despair, or whether she had accidently been caught by the raging waters nobody could be sure but she was missing that night. Next day the body, caught in the wreckage of a tree, was recovered from lower down the river.

The people at the farm where she worked laid her out in the barn, hanging up her sodden clothes on a nail, and covering the body with an old sheet. There she lay for several days while the local vicar tried to decide if she could be buried in hallowed ground, being almost certainly a suicide since nobody in their senses would have tried to cross the ford that day. Before he made up his mind the body had vanished! The sheet was still there, neatly folded on a box. Her soaking clothes were still hanging on the nail. But no Kitty. Just about a year later when the ford was swollen high Kitty's former lover, whilst attempting to cross on his horse, was thrown and dashed against the stones, suffering a mortal head injury. But before he died he managed to convey the information that a 'sarkless' woman had suddenly risen, white as a ghost from the brown water, and panicked his horse. That was the beginning of many drownings which only came to an end when the bridge was built, but the mystery of the missing corpse was never solved.

Product of Pain

KIRKHAM PRIORY

Approx. 4 miles

KIRKHAM PRIORY car park is reached by turning off the A64 York-Scarborough road at Whitwell-on-the-Hill and following the signposts to Kirkham. Leave the car park and cross the low pointed-arch stone bridge under which the River Derwent runs still and deep. Enter the nursery garden on your right and go through the gate at the end. Turn left to cross the railway line (observing British Rail's safety advice) Cross the fence ahead by a concrete stile and walk diagonally left up the slope to a gate. Go through this and follow the track to another gate which leads through Bellmire Hill Farm to Shepherdfields Lane. Cross the lane and follow the right hand side hedge towards the A64 ahead which you reach through a gap in the hedge.

Cross the A64 with care and bear left to the white railed fence and stone steps which mark a stile into a field where you follow the path up the right hand side. On your right is the church of St John the Evangelist at Whitwell-on-the-Hill.

Emerging onto the road, turn right up Whitwell's High Street — this was the Scarborough road before the dual carriageway was built. It is a far cry from London's Strand but the Strand's Law Courts and Whitwell's Church were built by the same man — G E Street.

The road, now known as Tout Hill, takes you back towards the A64. Just before reaching this turn left between two stone pillars. This is Whitwell Road which passes through Bank Wood. Almost immediately you are at the brow of Welburn Bank where there are a further two stone pillars. Gravity will now impel you down the slope into the picturesque village of Welburn with the curiously named Chanting Hill Farm at the cross roads. Just beyond, to the left, is the *Crown & Cushion* pub whose curious name was gained in 1851 when the Earl of Carlisle invited Queen Victoria to stay at Castle Howard.

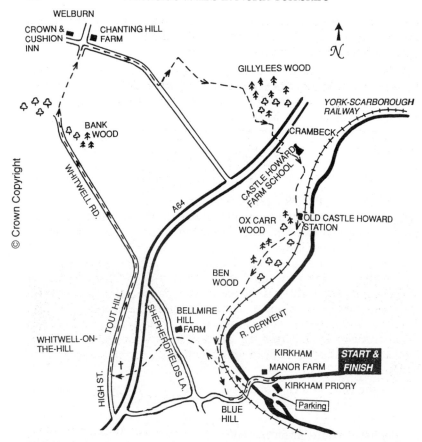

His preparations included the building of Castle Howard station: for
their part the villagers decorated the route she would take, including a
crown on a cushion outside the present pub. Interestingly there is no
longer a *Black Bull* pub in the village. The reason? Apparently the avidly
teetotal Countess of Carlisle descended one night from Castle Howard
and turned out all the customers from the pub and announced it would
never again serve alcohol. From then on it was known as *Temperance
Inn* — today it is the Temperance Farm.

Leave Welburn by turning right and follow the lane back towards the
A64. After the lane bends right take the bridleway on the left just past
some houses and, after about a hundred yards, turn right at the arrow
and follow the right hand side of the hedge. At the corner of the field
head across the open field, taking a line between two pylons to reach

the corner of the quaintly named Gillylees Wood. A yellow arrow on a green plate here points right, and by following the edge of the wood you reach the A64 which you cross again.

Walk to your right for a few yards before descending past Castle Howard Farm School. On your right is a path which you follow past the school greenhouses. Hereabouts, in 1858, were found Roman remains and coins.

Kirkham Priory across the River Derwent weir

At the foot of the slope the path enters woodland as it bears right along Kirkham Valley. Mature trees in Ox Carr Wood have been felled to be replaced by new saplings where the path follows a high level parallel to the railway before dropping down left to the old Castle Howard station. The line closed to passengers in 1930, and entirely in 1959. The magnificent stone structure, with its balcony almost brushing passing trains, must have been an expensive welcome for the Queen — for this was its original purpose.

From Station House cross the roadway and take the path through Ben Wood. As you approach your setting out point you will be rewarded with a second glimpse — like the re-run of a favourite old film — of the environs of Kirkham Priory. Its tumbled-down stones marking its skeletal remains on a carpet of springy turf is a reminder of the daily round of the twelfth century Augustinian monks and the Dissolution of 1539. The mossy steps of the cross just outside the gateway are, according to tradition in an old manuscript, associated with the event which led to the founding of the priory by Walter Espec, Lord of Helmsley. He had, we are told, an only son named Walter, who was fond of riding with excessive speed. One day, when galloping at a great pace, his horse stumbled near a small stone and young Espec was brought violently to the ground breaking his neck and leaving his father childless. The grief-stricken parent is said to have found

Gatehouse and base of cross at Kirkham Priory

consolation by the founding of three abbeys, one of them being at Kirkham where the fatal accident took place. The very stone that the unfortunate boy struck in falling is, according to the legend, incorporated in the base of the cross.

Alas, this picturesque story lacks confirmation from other sources but Walter Espec definitely founded the priory for Augustinian monks early in the twelfth century.

The path now keeps company with the railway and river as they swing in a broad arc until you reach Blue Hill where you bear left to cross the river once more back to the priory.

Palace of Destiny

BISHOPTHORPE

Approx. 6 miles

PARK IN YORK in St Georges Field car park betwixt the Rivers Foss and Ouse. Leave the car park and turn left over Skeldergate Bridge. Opened to pedestrians on 1 January 1881 and to carriages on 10 March, this bridge was not fully completed until 1882 and it cost £67,000. Tolls were removed in 1914. Take the slope to your left down the side of the bridge and turn right at the bottom before walking forward with Clementhorpe on your right and the Ouse on your left. A distillery once occupied this site which about 1850 became a fertiliser works. From here too ran the daily steam packet boats to Hull up to about 1870. They made the journey in about eight hours and returned according to the tide at Hull. The first of these packets was the *Waterloo* which ran a trial trip on 25 April 1816.

Walk forward and you will soon see Rowntree Park on your right and a pleasant detour can be made around the gardens by horticultural enthusiasts. Ignore the road to your right at the end of Terry Avenue and continue forward along the banks of the river. You are here at Nun Ings with Fulford Ings on the opposite side. Derived from an old English word meaning 'foul ford', the village of Fulford has long military associations dating back to the erection of cavalry barracks in 1795/6. It was also the terminus of the famous ride attributed to Dick Turpin but in fact performed by another highwayman, William Nevison who was hanged at York Tyburn on 4 May 1684.

Nun Ings leads you into Middlethorpe Ings which is reputedly haunted by a white headless lady. Many years ago she is said to have been cruelly murdered and decapitated when out for an evening stroll. Ever since, she haunts the banks looking for her murderer and she is said to be less offensive to residents than strangers. Continue forward until your path is barred and you are obliged to turn right through a gateway and along a short fenced pathway which brings you to

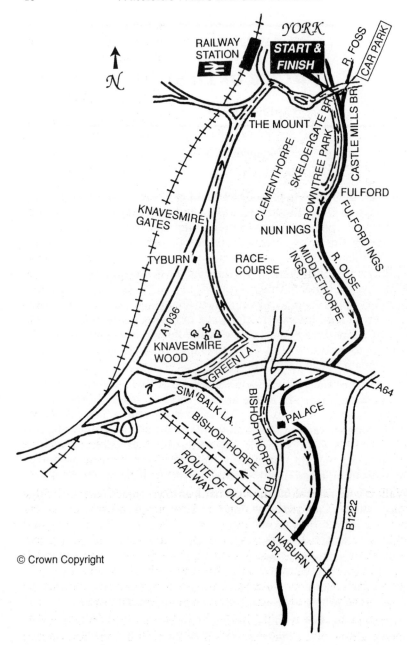

© Crown Copyright

The Gatehouse to Bishopthorpe Palace

Bishopthorpe Road — at which point you leave the city boundary.

Turn left and walk around the perimeter of the Archbishop of York's Bishopthorpe Palace gardens, past the imposing gatehouse, and turn left at Chantry Lane to return to the riverside. Archbishop Gray purchased St Andrewthorpe early in the thirteenth century, called it Bishopthorpe, and attached it to the See of York. The present building and fanciful gatehouse are due principally to Archbishop Drummond who died in 1766. The Great Hall was the scene of the sentencing to death of Archbishop Scrope for joining the rebellion against King Henry VI headed by the Mowbrays and Percys. Lord Chief Justice Gascoigne refused to sentence His Grace and a lawyer named Fulthorpe pronounced judgement at the instigation of the King.

Walk to your right along the river bank until you reach Naburn Bridge which was built to carry the London/Edinburgh railway line across the river. Some 26 feet above summer river level, it is 280 feet long and originally consisted of two spans, one moveable and one fixed. Immediately before the bridge bear right up the slope and sharp left upwards to enter the York/Selby Railway Path where you turn right to cross the bridge over the road. Walk forward, skirting Bishopthorpe village, until you reach the right-hand exit to Sim Balk Lane.

Turn right down Sim Balk Lane and look for a metal stile on your left which gives access to Green Lane. Follow the well-defined route along the edge of fields and skirting Knavesmire Wood to join the racecourse.

From here follow the left hand circuit until you reach the junction of Tadcaster Road (A1036) and Knavesmire Road at Knavesmire Gates. On your left is the site of the York Tyburn where many criminals and others met their end. Walk forward up The Mount to the junction of Scarcroft Road on your right. Turn down here until you reach Bishopthorpe Road where you turn left and continue forward to rejoin Skeldergate Bridge and the start of the walk

Bishopthorpe Palace reflected in the River Ouse

Fish for the King

YORK

Approx. 5 miles. Return by bus.

YORK is the confluence of two rivers — the Ouse and the Foss — and while the majority of people are familiar with the former, the latter is largely ignored so it is particularly attractive for those who want a waterside walk without tourist crowds. Parking is conveniently available in St George's Field alongside Skeldergate Bridge over the Ouse.

Leave the car park at Blue Bridge over the Foss and walk up the left hand side of the Foss Basin to Castle Mills lock. Turn right across Castle Mills Bridge and enjoy the view upstream as the river bends around

The River Foss at Monk Bridge, York

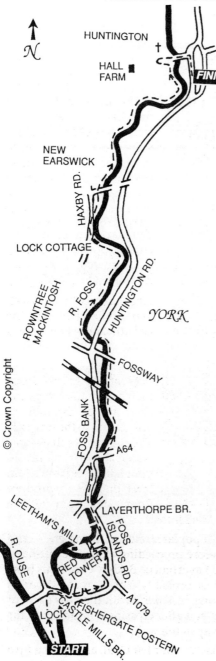

the Castle Museum with Raindale Mill at its foot. There was no bridge over the Foss here for many centuries but a wooden footbridge was built at some time in the seventeenth century, being replaced in 1733 by a larger wooden structure across which horses — but not carts — as well as pedestrians could cross. The first stone bridge was erected about 1793 when the Foss Navigation Company was formed, the River Foss canalised, and Castle Mills lock constructed. This bridge was incorporated into the present structure in 1876.

A few yards to your left is Fishergate Postern where you ascend the city walls and, keeping right, walk round to Red Tower where you descend. The Red Tower was doubtless so called because of the contrast between the colour of its bricks and the white of the walls. Probably erected in the sixteenth century, it has served many purposes including being a manufactory of brimstone, and a pigsty! For centuries the Red Tower stood on the waters edge, for many acres around were submerged under the King's Fishpool of Foss — an artificial mere designed

Leetham's mill alongside the River Foss, York

to provide a water-filled castle moat and a royal preserve for fish throughout medieval times when church laws caused fish to be an important part of diet. In 1221 ten bream from the *vivario de Fosse* were presented as a gift to the Archbishop of York by the Sheriff on mandate of the king, and in 1293 a Thomas Warthill was gaoled for poaching from the King's Fish Pond. York Corporation purchased the fishing rights in 1854 and immediately reclaimed a large area of land which was followed by the construction of Foss Islands Road.

Turn left between the flats of Rosemary Place then right into Navigation Road and go through the opening on to the towpath. The impressive five-storey waterside structure to your left is Leetham's Mill built in 1898 to produce flour, and from 1981 a storage warehouse for Rowntree Mackintosh.

Turn right along the towpath — a poplar stretch with anglers — and pass through a concrete tunnel before proceeding along the left-hand pavement of Foss Islands Road to Layerthorpe Bridge. Cross this busy traffic point with care to what is probably York's most deserted footpath and proceed forward along Foss Bank with the Foss on your right. A tree-lined footpath greets you after crossing a bridge over the A64 and passing through a gateway in the wall.

Walk along the path with the Foss on your left until, after going up a stone staircase and through some portals, you cross Fossway and then Huntington Road at some traffic lights before going through a gap in a wall to the riverside path. The former Yearsley Lock is passed and the dominating factory and headquarters of Rowntree Mackintosh as the river keeps company with Huntington Road.

After about half a mile a brief flirtation of a few yards with a roadside path brings you to Lock Cottage with a New Earswick sign and path to the right which returns you to the riverside and past a nature reserve. Continue along the river bank to Huntington where a lane leads from All Saints Church into the village from where there is a frequent bus service back to York.

In Memory of Marian

THE POPPLETONS

7 miles

THE POPPLETONS — Upper and Nether — signal the departure of Suburbia and the arrival of verdant countryside some four miles west of York off the A59 towards Harrogate. Upper Poppleton has preserved its two greens and majestic 64 foot high maypole, maintaining a tradition with this 1½ ton red, white and blue striped monster which goes back to 1830 according to parish records. And at Nether Poppleton where the River Ouse, banked by broad-leaved chestnuts, purple beeches, dark-hued Scots firs and drooping willows, meets the road is the unusual peace memorial of a rocky cairn strewn with flowers and commemorating twelve villagers who gave their lives in two World Wars.

Join the bridle path here which follows the river as it gouges out a channel through the rich alluvial plain. Hereabouts Prince Rupert brought an army across the river during the War of the Roses.

A stile enables you to cross the stream (the Foss) before you continue along the river bank. On the opposite side are the estates of Beningborough Hall, home of a major exhibition from the National Portrait Gallery, and the setting for a melodrama that occurred around 1776 (see panel, page 50).

Continue forward, passing Red House School on your left. Red House, very much wrapped up in the history of the Civil War, is said to have accommodated Prince Rupert and Charles I, as well as other notables. Preserved in the magnificent old chapel is the original staircase from the main house. A fascinating description of it is provided in the diary of Sir Henry Slingsby who wrote:

The staircase yt leads to the painted chamber was furnished ye last year by John Gowland, carpenter at Poppleton. Ye stair is about 5 feet within ye sides in wideness: ye post 8 inches square:

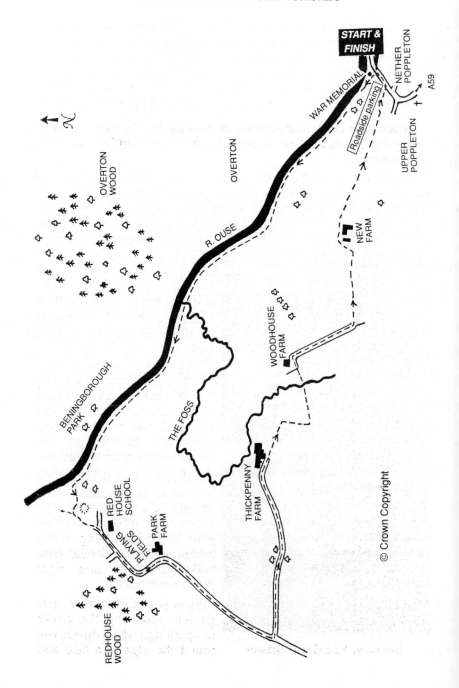

N

OVERTON WOOD

OVERTON

R. OUSE

BENINGBOROUGH PARK

THE FOSS

RED HOUSE SCHOOL

PARK FARM

PLAYING FIELDS

REDHOUSE WOOD

WOODHOUSE FARM

THICKPENNY FARM

NEW FARM

WAR MEMORIAL

Roadside parking

START & FINISH

NETHER POPPLETON

UPPER POPPLETON

A59

© Crown Copyright

upon every post a crest is set of my special friends and of my brothers-in-law and upon that post yt bears up the half pace yt leads into the painted chamber there sits a blackamore cast in led by Andrew Carne, a Dutchman, who also cast in stone ye statue of ye horse in the garden. Ye blackamore sits holding in either hand a candlestick to set a candle in to give light in ye staircase.

The fourteen crests still survive, as does the blackamore — minus hands and candle holders — reputed to be the earliest lead statue in the country.

Past the school go through the gate and turn sharp left along the floodbank away from the river. On the right is a water authority lagoon from which water is pumped to Eccup reservoir which serves Leeds.

Statue in Red House School

Follow the embankment, keeping a hedge on your left, to a stile in the left hand corner of the field. Join the lane and proceed past Red House playing fields. After about a mile turn left at a dormer bungalow to go over a cattle grid.

The track passes over Thickpenny Farm and, keeping this on your left, go through a gate to cross some flat farmland with rich soil producing fine crops and bisected by the meandering waters of the Foss.

At the end of the field turn left and cross the track to walk straight ahead, keeping the hedge and a modern house on your left, before going over a bridge and stile to derelict farm buildings. Then turn right down a cart track.

When you reach a metal gate go left, following the public footpath sign which directs you round the edge of a field and over a stile, past a Dutch barn and left along the back of New Farm. Passing an old petrol pump of indeterminate age you go straight ahead to cross two fields, or follow the embankments, to return to your starting point at Nether Poppleton.

The Drama of Beningborough Hall.

This tale concerns a wicked steward who contrived the dastardly murder of the virtuous house keeper.

The Hall was tenanted by a Mr and Mrs Giles Earle who seem to have lived abroad much of the time. So Marian, the housekeeper, was not surprised when two men arrived with instructions to pack all valuables into two boxes and await forwarding instructions. She arranged to store the boxes in the cottage of gamekeeper Martin Giles to whom she was engaged.

The steward of the Hall, Philip Laurie, discovered where the valuables were held and enlisted the aid of a local layabout called William Vasey in a plan to steal them. Knowing that Marian, who had previously spurned his advances, took an evening stroll along a beech avenue down by the river, he hid behind a tree and pounced on the unsuspecting girl before strangling her and throwing the body into the river.

Suicide was assumed at first, but imprints of boots in the mud and behind the tree suggested foul play. Paradoxically, suspicion fell on her lover, perhaps due to his secretive behaviour as custodian of the valuables. Taking advantage of this, Laurie and Vasey decided to steal the valuables and murder Martin. With Laurie keeping watch outside, Vasey broke into the cottage but Martin was awakened and managed to raise the alarm which was answered by other servants — including Laurie! Vasey was captured, committed to York Castle, and charged with burglary and attempted murder.

Word of the incident reached Mrs Earle who travelled back to Beningborough Hall and, for some reason, suspected Laurie whom she dismissed with the news that Vasey was about to make a full confession. Laurie admitted his involvement but, finding no forgiveness tried, unsuccessfully, to shoot Mrs Earle and then blew out his own brains. Vasey was tried, condemned, made a full confession, and was hanged at York Tyburn on 18 August 1760.

Soon afterwards, a pale, neat figure, with shoulders bowed and head bent was seen walking along the banks of the Ouse by many people. This tall, statuesque lady, eventually disappeared into the churchyard where the unfortunate Marian was buried.

Timeless Illusions

KNARESBOROUGH

Approx. 1, 3 or 3½ miles

PARK IN KNARESBOROUGH MARKET PLACE, notable for its picturesque roof-tops and ancient foundations. First mentioned in 1206, the market has officially been held on Wednesday ever since 1310 when Edward II's charter made the inhabitants Free Burghers. Entirely cobbled until 1963, a remnant of the old cobblestones can be seen around the market cross (the base of which dates from 1709). Two notable buildings in the Market Place are "Ye Oldest Chymist Shoppe", in continuous use as a pharmacy since 1720 (the box windows on legs of Chinese Chippendale were added in 1760) and the former Town Hall (now Castle Court shopping arcade), built in 1862. Note the balcony from which electioneering speeches were made until 1885 when Knaresborough was disfranchised after sending a total of 187 members to Parliament since 1553.

Keeping Castle Court on your left, leave the market place and make for Castle Yard, passing between the modern police station on your left and the Free Dispensary built in 1853. Continue forward until you reach Knaresborough Castle. Started soon after the Norman Conquest by Serlo de Burgh, the majority of the ruins date from the fourteenth century when there was a massive keep and twelve towers. Interesting residents of the castle include the murderers of Thomas à Beckett; King John; Edward III and Queen Philippa; their son John of Gaunt, the Duke of Lancaster (it has belonged to the Duchy of Lancaster since 1372); Thomas Chaucer (son of the poet); and Richard II (imprisoned here just before his death in 1399). Knaresborough Castle has been attacked only twice, in 1317 and in 1644, shortly after the Battle of Marston Moor, when it was captured by the Roundheads. Two years later, Cromwell ordered its demolition.

Notice the twin towers and the ruins of the Barbican Gate, the main entrance. The King's Chamber and Dungeon can be visited. In a cottage

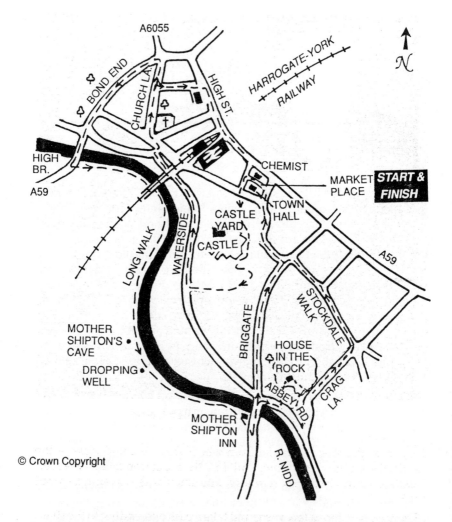

© Crown Copyright

near here the famous road builder Blind Jack Metcalfe was born in 1717.

Just beyond the castle pause to enjoy the spectacular view of the River Nidd flowing through its fairy-tale gorge, with the old town rising in tiers above it. Notice the railway viaduct and the parish church. The riverside woodland (a glorious sight in autumn) known as the Long Walk, was planted by the Slingsby family in 1739. If you have time, look round the Old Courthouse (museum) and certainly walk to the

The ruins of Knaresborough Castle

point near the War Memorial from which there is a fine view of the Castle Mill on the river below. Built in 1791 as a cotton mill it was soon adapted for the local flax industry, and linen was woven here until 1972.

Retrace your steps a few yards and take a path descending to the river. This brings you to Waterside. Turn right and walk as far as the viaduct, rebuilt in 1851 after the original one, almost completed, had collapsed into the river (11 March 1848). Just beyond the viaduct you will see a wall on your right, part of the town gibbet on which the body of the schoolmaster Eugene Aram was displayed in 1759 after he had been hanged in York for the murder of Daniel Clark. (N.B.the gibbet actually stood in a field just beyond the *Mother Shipton Inn*). Continue along Waterside as far as the Olde Manor House, reputed to have been the hunting lodge of King John, and turn right up the cobbled street known as Water Bag Bank, so called because the town's water supply was once carried up here in leather bags on horseback. Before you go up the hill notice the elegant gas lamp dating from 1824 and, on your right, the thatched Manor Cottage, possibly the oldest house in Knaresborough.

Railway viaduct over the River Nidd,

Turn sharp left at the top and walk towards the church, noting the grave-yard, landscaped in 1973, and above it, on the south-east side, the building (1741) which once housed King James's Grammar School, founded in 1616 on the same site. Before entering the parish church observe the handsome exterior with the distinctive little 'candle-snuffer' spire and the old clock inscribed with St Paul's exhortation to make the best use of time. Inside you will see architecture from successive periods — the Norman church dating from 1100 (in the chancel), the early thirteenth century chapels, and the fifteenth century nave. Notice the font with its ponderous seventeenth century cover. Visit the Roundell chapel (south) which contains Early English arches, decorated sedilia and Easter sepulchre. The Slingsby Chapel contains tombs of the distinguished family, including a prominent one with full-length figures of Sir Francis Slingsby and his lady, Mary. Sir Francis (d.1600 aged 78) served with distinction under Henry VIII, Mary Tudor and Queen Elizabeth I. Do not miss the very simple tomb just in front of this. Covered by a slab of black marble (brought from St Robert's

Priory) it contains the remains of Sir Henry Slingsby who fought at
Marston Moor and was later beheaded(1658) "on account of his fidelity
to his king ... by order of the tyrant Cromwell." (part of the Latin
inscription). A member of this family, incidentally, helped to turn
Knaresborough into a spa long before Harrogate, when William
Slingsby of Bilton Hall discovered the Tewit Well on rough moorland
(now Harrogate's Stray and no longer part of Knaresborough) in 1571.

As you leave the church turn sharp right at the door and proceed
down Church Lane. Look out for the second gate on your right. Go
through this and enjoy the stately view of Knaresborough House built
in 1768. It was the home of Thomas Collins, Vicar of Knaresborough
from 1735 until his death in 1788 and later of Lady Evelyn Collins (a
cousin of Winston Churchill) who sold it to Knaresborough Council in
1952.

☐ The walk could be completed here by walking through the
  grounds of Knaresborough House to the High Street where you
  turn right and go up the hill back to the Market Place.

☐ To see more of Knaresborough return through the gate to Church
  Lane and continue to the end, noting the well-preserved Tudor St
  John's House. At this point turn left and proceed down Low Bond
  End.

Across the road you will see the Dower House of the Slingsby Family
(Tudor interior). Beyond this are the grounds of Conyngham Hall. On

Objects being petrified in the Knaresborough Dropping Well

The Market Square and the Old Town Hall, Knaresborough

your left is St Mary's Catholic Church (1831, interior modernised 1973). Cross High Bridge, enlarged in 1773, and look for the Queen Victoria Jubilee Fountain (1887) which once conveyed spa water from Bilton.

Now turn left to enter the grounds of the Dropping Well, making sure you buy a ticket (Open daily Easter to 31 October, otherwise Sundays only, 10.00 to 16.00). Do not be put off by the name "The Long Walk". The short stroll through this woodland is made all the more delightful by views of the town across the river. Soon you will reach the famous Dropping Well. John Leland, antiquary to Henry VIII, noted its petrifying properties as long ago as 1540. He did not, however, mention Mother Shipton's Cave nearby, where the prophetess is said to have been born in 1488. Mother Shipton was certainly not a witch and her most spectacular prophecies (e.g. about the end of the world) are alleged to be nineteenth century forgeries. Before leaving this romantic grotto dip your hand in the ice-cold water of the Wishing Well.

Continue to the far end of the wood, emerging at the seventeenth century *Mother Shipton Inn*. Beware of the traffic, then turn left over Low Bridge (enlarged 1779) passing Bridge House(about 1745).

- ☐ If you wish, the walk can now be completed by climbing up Briggate, then turning left down Cheapside for the Market Place.
- ☐ For an alternative route to the top turn right along Abbey Road, named after the Trinitarian Priory which once stood near the riverside hermitage of St Robert.

A gate on the left gives access to the Chapel of Our Lady of the Crag, a small shrine cut out of the rock by John the Mason about 1408 (key available from the house). You can now climb the steps to the House in the Rock (for which there is an admission fee) constructed between 1770 and 1786 by Thomas Hill for his wife and sixteen children. Hill, who was a naval man, got the idea of building into the rock during a trip to Turkey. A visiting aristocrat, the Duchess Margaret Buccleugh, persuaded Hill to build a four-storey instead of a one-storey home. And is because of her involvement that the house is often known as Fort Montague, the family name of the Duchess.

If this quaint house is open it is well worth a visit and you will enjoy a superb view. However, if it is closed, or you prefer to omit it, carry on a little further along Abbey Road and take the footpath on your left. In either case you will emerge onto Crag Lane — turn left along this, then left along Stockale Walk (which becomes Windsor Lane) to return to the town centre.

The Downfall of Eugene Aram

Eugene Aram was born at Ramsgill in Nidderdale some time late in the September of 1704 and as a result of a brilliant intellect and untiring application he became something of a scholar. He worked both as a schoolmaster and as steward of a small estate at Knaresborough. As such he would seem to be an unlikely associate of Richard Houseman, said to have been repulsive in aspect and character, Henry Terry, landlord of the *Barrel Inn*, and Daniel Clark. But what sort of man was Aram himself? Some accounts say he was a sensitive man. Others describe him as a recluse who found few people worthy of his conversation. One of those rare exceptions was young Daniel Clark. Perhaps it was money that brought him and the impecunious schoolmaster together for, in addition to inheriting a prosperous shoe business from his father, his recently married wife brought him a handsome dowry. On the strength of this Clark bought large quantities of goods on credit, borrowed silver tankards and other articles from innkeepers and told of arranging a sumptuous feast for his friends.

Clark left home on 7 February 1744 intent on visiting his pregnant wife and staying with relatives in a nearby village, but he never arrived. He was seen that night in the company of Houseman and Aram — and then no more. Missing too were his money and newly-acquired goods. He had apparently decamped and his creditors were quickly on his track, offering a reward of £15 for information. A search was made and some of the missing goods — velvets and drapery — were dug up in Aram's garden, while others were found in Houseman's possession. Aram was in debt to a Mr Norton who was persuaded to have him arrested so that he could be held and duly charged with complicity in Clark's frauds. But to everyone's amazement Aram discharged the debt and avoided arrest. Furthermore he shortly afterwards paid off a considerable mortgage on a house in Ripon left to him by his father.

The intended prosecution fell through and Aram left Knaresborough and his wife, for London. He filled various posts for the next fourteen years, finally settling at King's Lynn as a teacher. But on 1 August 1758 a labourer digging for stones on Thistle Hill near Knaresborough unearthed a wooden chest containing a skeleton, and memories of Daniel Clark were quickly revived. An inquest was held at which it was discovered that Aram's wife, her husband and Houseman had been with Clark on the fateful day he had disappeared. Houseman was brought before the Coroner and on being committed to York Castle on suspicion of murder "confessed" that Aram had murdered Clark. Aram was arrested and brought back to Yorkshire but denied he killed Clark and accused Houseman and Terry, the publican. At the trial Houseman was acquitted for lack of evidence whereupon he turned King's Evidence and repeated his accusation against Aram. It was hardly answered when the schoolmaster read his written defence, a somewhat florid but ingenious document which has won a certain fame. He was convicted and sentenced to death but he tried to escape the gallows by cutting his arms with a razor. He was hastily patched up and taken to the gallows, his body being returned to Knaresborough to hang in chains. For more than a century after his execution controversy raged and pamphlets were penned asserting his villainy or innocence. And as a local poet put it:

The gibbet clasped its victim fast
And his bones bleached in the wintry blast;
His passions brought a death of shame,
His learning gave him endless fame.

Solitude of the Spa

HARROGATE

Approx. 5 miles

THIS FIVE MILE WALK, that stays within two miles of the bustling town centre and can mostly be covered without encountering a single car, may sound impossible; but it exists. Along the way are some of the best kept gardens in England, quiet pine woods, a spectacular viewpoint from the top of a crag, and a fourteenth century packhorse bridge.

The walk begins outside Harrogate's Royal Pump Room Museum at the bottom of Valley Gardens, just a few minutes from the bus and train stations; there are a considerable number of on-street parking spots in the vicinity. Take the path up the centre of the gardens alongside a stream until a wide circular area emerges with a pool and a statue in the centre. It is here that thirty-six of the mineral springs that made Harrogate so famous as a spa emerge into what is known as Bogs Field. Some of the cover plates can still be seen.

The route carries on up the valley, past the tennis courts and the miniature golf course, until the crucifix war memorial is reached. Here the path splits three ways as it enters the pine woods. These cover about 65 acres and were planted in 1769 as part of the King's Plantation. Take the middle path.

After crossing Harlow Moor Road, follow the sign marked Crag Lane along a path which swings left to skirt an open grassed area with seats around the perimeter. After encountering further woods you will be rewarded with panoramic views across the valley. To the north west is the Army Apprentices College with its distinctive tent-like chapels and behind that can sometimes be glimpsed the grey outline of Great Whernside even though it is some twenty miles distant. The path emerges on Crag Lane, outside the trial ground of the Northern Horticultural Society, Harlow Car Gardens. There is a striking contrast between the rough expanse of pine gorse and heath which make up the moor and the manicured lawns, flower beds and rock gardens of the other side of the lane.

Turn right down Crag Lane until after a few yards the drive of the *Harrogate Arms* is met on the left. This pubs boasts thousands of beer mats from all over the world which are stuck across the ceiling. Go down the drive and through the car park to meet a wire fence. Then bear right through the woodland to a bird feeding station and hide on

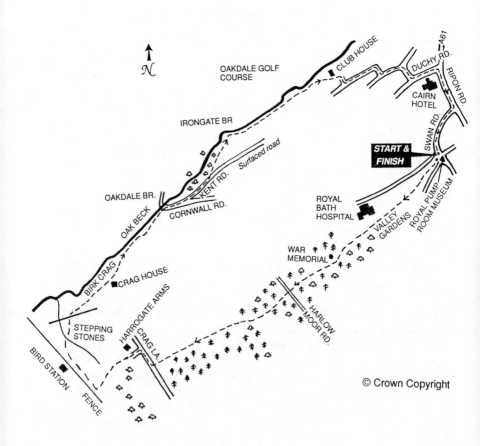

© Crown Copyright

the left. At this point look carefully on the right for a faint path which bears left down to some stepping stones (a little further on there are some rough stone steps which join this path). Cross the beck and turn left onto a path which goes over some duck boards to a fence. Go through the stile in this fence and turn right up the path which leads to Birk Crag. From the top boulder of the crag there are superb views. Along the line of the ridge can be seen the Hambledon Hills and, in good weather conditions, the White Horse of Kilburn more than 20 miles away. The rocks that make up the crag are part of a fault called the Harrogate Anticline — they also surface at Alms Cliff Crag, to the south. Over 150 feet below lies the Oak Beck, a tiny channel considering the width and depth of the valley which it would seem to have cut when the overflow waters from the glacial Lake Washburn ran down it.

Leaving Crag House at the top follow the path along the top of the ridge before descending by stone steps to the beck. Turn right and follow the beck to Oakdale Bridge. Ornithologists should be pleased to find dippers, grey and pied wagtails, tree-creepers, several of the finches, yellow-hammers and wood pigeon hereabouts as sometimes are the cuckoo and tawny owl.

Panel in Harrogate Pump Room

Take the road to the right up the hill a short way before bearing left along the unsurfaced Kent Road which joins a surfaced road. Pass the new bridge on your left which services a private housing development. After about a hundred yards you will see, near some spruce trees, a pointer on your left. The path goes between two houses down to Iron Gate Bridge. Well shaded in branches, this three-foot wide structure, which now goes absolutely nowhere, is a remarkable survival of a fourteenth century packhorse bridge.

From here on the walk follows the clearly visible track down the right hand bank of Oak Beck with the golf course across on the other side. Just before the golf club house climb up steeply to emerge in the car park.

Turn right out of the car park up Oakdale Glen and at the top turn left and follow the road to Kent Road where you turn left. Then turn right into Wood View and at the end turn left into Duchy Road opposite the Cairn Hotel. At the junction with Ripon road turn right and stroll down the hill to Swan Road which swings right in a gentle arc back to the Royal Pump Room Museum where you started.

Mystery of the Marker

RIPON

Approx. 5 miles

NORTH BRIDGE, RIPON, carrying the A61 over the River Ure, is the starting point for this walk. There is convenient parking space in Magdalens Road.

Walk a short distance along Magdalens Road and you will see a path to your left which leads down to the banks of the meandering river. On the opposite bank is the village of Sharow where legend has it that Lewis Carroll first saw eight-year-old Mary Badcock, the girl on whom he modelled the character of Alice. He persuaded her father, who was a canon of Ripon Cathedral, to lend him her picture which he passed to the illustrator Sir John Tenniel and she became immortalised as Alice in Wonderland.

Marker on the bank of the River Skell, Ripon

Walk along the right bank of the river. As you approach the confluence with the River Skell the path "cuts the corner" and you bear right to continue along the north bank of the

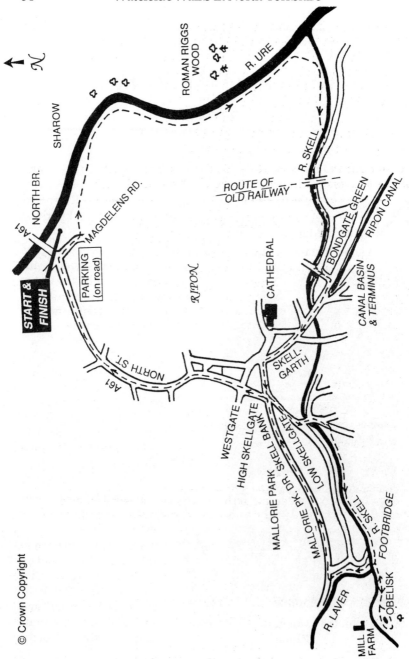

© Crown Copyright

river. As the path crosses a green sward look to your right for the stepping stones sheltered by a willow tree and cross to the opposite bank. Turn right and go under the bridge which formerly carried a railway line. Continue forward, cross the river at the weir, then back again by a bridge to Bondgate Bridge.

Soon you will be greeted by the bulk of the cathedral towering over riverside houses, a weir next to a footbridge, and the adjacent *Alma Inn* where you turn left to join Bondgate Green almost opposite the terminal basin of the Ripon Canal with its *Navigation Inn*.

Turn right and cross the River Skell before bearing left up Skellgarth to the junction with Water Skellgate. Keep to the left when High

---

Hornblowing at Ripon

Every night of the year, without fail, a horn is blown, first at the four corners of the obelisk in Ripon to set the watch, and then outside the house of the Mayor. This ceremony commemorates the time in the Middle Ages when Ripon's first citizen, the Wakeman, was responsible for crime prevention in the city from 9.00 pm until dawn, and had to compensate victims of burglary. The Wakeman had constables to patrol the streets, and also had the right to levy a rate on houses according to the number of their doors — fourpence a year for two doors and twopence a year for one door.

Although the office of Wakeman became that of Mayor in 1604, and the maintenance of law and order became the responsibility of the police force in the nineteenth century, the importance of the horn in the civic life of the town continues.

In addition to the nightly blasts it was ordered that it should be carried in front of the Mayor — so that the townsfolk may see it — to church on five 'Horn Days': Candlemas, Easter Sunday, Wednesday in Rogation Week, the Sunday after Lammas and St Stephen's Day. And it is still borne in front of the Mayor when he attends the Cathedral on important festivals. A representation of a horn was long ago adopted as the town's unofficial coat of arms and it has become the symbol of Ripon.

The city has, in fact, four horns, the oldest of which is known as the Charter Horn, since, according to ancient tradition, it symbolised the granting of charter rights to Ripon in AD886. A second horn was acquired in 1690, and a third, purchased by the Mayor in 1865, is the one normally blown today. A fourth horn, given to the city in 1886, came from one of the beasts in the Chillingham herd of wild cattle in Northumberland.

Skellgate on the right joins Low Skellgate which you follow back over the River Skell. Take the right fork over the bridge and look for a gap in the wall. From here take the footpath along the bank of the river noting the footbridge just before the confluence with the River Laver on your right. A short distance past the footbridge (which you will cross later) you will come upon a stone column to which is fixed a metal plate inscribed:

RIPON NAVIGATION
1820
LEVEL OF THE SKELL CROOKS DAM
SEVEN FEET BELOW THIS
MARK —

The confluence of the Rivers Skell and Laver at Ripon

Despite the inscription its origins are shrouded in mystery and there are two theories for its existence. One view is that it once held water to feed to Ripon Canal on the east side of the city. A more likely explanation is that it was one of a series of reservoirs linking a millrace used to feed five water mills for grinding flour. This ran across the city from west to east crossing under High Skellgate by a conduit then opening out into a large pond, Water Skellgate, of today. On ran the water down the present Skellgarth, taking up the whole of the road's width, before flowing into the River Skell near the road bridge.

Retrace your steps past the confluence with the River Laver and turn left to cross the footbridge and follow the bankside footpath to Mallorie Park Drive where you turn right. With the park on your left proceed along Skell Bank to the junction with High Skellgate where you turn left. Cross Westgate to the Market Place with its famous cross at the foot of which the city hornblower maintains the ancient custom (see panel). Keep to the left hand side as you proceed up North Street which carries the A61 North Road in a continuous right hand curve to reach North Bridge from which you started.

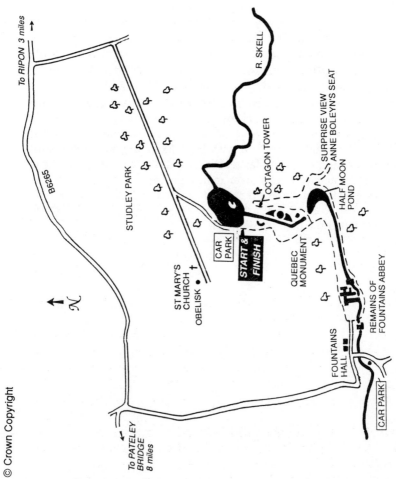

© Crown Copyright

Miles of Meditation

STUDLEY ROYAL AND FOUNTAINS ABBEY

Approx. 3 miles

TAKE THE B6265 FROM RIPON TOWARDS PATELEY BRIDGE and after about two miles you will see a sign on your left that directs you to the attractive village of Studley Royal. Go through here, and then, between the magnificent wrought ironwork of imposing gates, the road rises gently between a majestic avenue of limes to the skyline dominated by St Mary's church, built by William Burges in 1871-78.

On either side is the 400 acre Studley Royal Park where a herd of around 350 deer graze, mostly Fallow, Red and Manchurian Sika. The undulating ground is dotted with magnificent aged specimens of oak, lime, beech, sweet chestnut and wild cherry, as well as more modern plantings of pine, cedar and larch.

Continue along the road which soon branches left and skirts a glittering lake to reach the car park and the entrance to what is perhaps the most spectacular water garden in England and one of the few great Georgian green gardens to survive virtually unchanged.

We owe it all to John Aislabie, Chancellor of the Exchequer, whose political career came to an abrupt end with the collapse of the South Sea Bubble in 1720. After he had been released from the Tower of London, to which he had been committed on charges of 'infamous foolhardihood and corruption', resulting in disqualification for life from public office, he withdrew to Studley Royal where all his energies were channelled into the improvement of the estate until his death in 1742.

Aislabie inherited the estate in 1699 when the steep sided Skell Valley was still untamed. During the first phase of its transformation he canalised the turbulent river to run down the centre of the vale. Sparse records indicate that for a decade from 1716 about a hundred men directed by Aislabie's gardener, William Fisher, laboured at the basic engineering of the garden and planted trees on the steep valley sides, with Scots Pine romantically crowning the ridges.

In 1732 building began of the 'Temples' — of Fame and Piety —, the Octagon tower, the Rustic Bridge and the Serpentine Tower, all of which were completed before Aislabie's death.

The Serpentine Tunnel, which leads to the Octagon Tower, is said to be evidence of John Aislabie's sense of humour. Only just wide enough to admit a coach and horses, it contains a fiendish bend which dramatically disguises its shortness and still calls forth requests for lights from nervous visitors — just as it inspired Gothic terrors in visiting ladies whose screams no doubt delighted Aislabie.

Fountains Abbey

The pillars of the Temple of Fame may be further illustrations of his eccentricity because to all appearances they are of stone, but tap them and you will know that they are timber.

But nothing can detract from the magnificent landscape that was looked upon as the 'wonder of the North' and inspired such writers as Philip York to record in his *Travel Journal* of 1744:

"Imagine rocks covered with wood, sometimes perpendicularly steep and craggy, or others descending in slopes to beautiful lawns and parterres, water thrown into twenty different shapes".

Aislabie's son William bought the abbey ruins from John Michael Messenger in 1786 and also took possession of Fountains Hall, built from abbey stone by Sir Stephen Proctor about 1600. William liked his landscapes to be tidy, and he undoubtedly saved what was left of the abbey by clearing out the trees rooted in its walls.

In 1966 it was purchased by the West Yorkshire County Council, and in 1983 the National Trust acquired the estate before embarking on a major scheme of restoration and conservation to return Studley to its former glory.

The water garden occupies about 150 of the 760 acres of the present estate and the walk starts by following the canal, with views over the yew hedges. At the end is the rustic bridge, added in the 1730s, and if you look down to the left you will see the only stone statuary in the garden. This depicts the giant Anteus, who was practically invincible because contact with the ground gave him strength, and Hercules, who has managed to lift him up and is squeezing him to death.

When you bear left over the bridge you will pass the curious feature known as the Quebec Monument. An explanation of any association seems lost in the mists of antiquity, but it was the custom at one time on 13 September each year for two small cannon to be fired to commemorate the anniversary of the capture of Quebec and the death of General Wolfe in 1759. The whole tangled area to the left of the path was originally a wilderness garden with a small lake.

Swinging round the semi-circle of the water garden the path now provides the best place to appreciate the geometric layout and the placing of statues. In the centre of the Moon Pond, Neptune has pride of place, flanked on either side at the end of the crescent ponds by Endymion and Bacchus.

On your right, overlooking the water garden, is the Temple of Piety backed by yews, Scots pine and beeches. Designed as a cool garden house on the shady side of the valley, it was originally dedicated to Hercules — whose labours could be compared with Aislabie's own labours in the construction of the garden. William renamed it as a symbol of filial piety soon after his father's death. Species of yew, box, guelder rose, juniper and sweet-briar have been replanted on the steep banks where the path climbs towards the rocky outcrop.

Through the dramatically twisting Serpentine Tunnel the path sweeps round to the right to the Octagon Tower, built about 1728 in severe Classical style, with parapet, pinnacles and porch added about ten

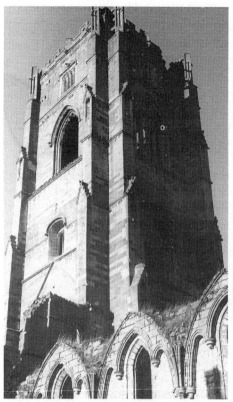

Central Tower. Fountains Abbey

years later. Before the trees matured there were superb views over Ripon Cathedral to the 25 miles distant Cleveland Hills, but nowadays the views are down onto the water garden and across the valley.

Meandering along the top of the valley, and through beeches, yews and Scots pine, the path reaches the rotunda called the Temple of Fame affording another good viewpoint. With trees crowding in on either side there is no warning of what to expect when you reach the climax of this high path — Anne Boleyn's Seat. Originally built in the late eighteenth century, but reconstructed several times since, it is the vantage point to John Aislabie's surprise view of Fountains Abbey, rising serenely from the banks of the River Skell far below. The scene is as impressive now as it was some two centuries ago.

Descending to the right into the valley again the path skirts Half Moon Pond and bears left up the romantically landscaped valley of the Skell with its informal sweep of grass. Robin Hood's Well on the right usually gets scant attention in competition with the dramatic views of the abbey framed in the woods on the valley sides.

The abbey itself was the product of a dispute at St Mary's Abbey, York which resulted in a riot in October 1132. Thirteen monks were exiled and given protection by Archbishop Thurstan at his palace in Ripon. From there, on 27 December, they made their way three miles up the River Skell to the site he had given them, but which was described as a place 'more fit for wild beasts than man to inhabit'.

Practising austere principles, and using lay brothers for routine jobs, the monks devoted themselves unreservedly to their life of prayer and meditation. By the middle of the thirteenth century Fountains was one of the richest religious houses in England, with vast flocks of sheep grazing huge estates stretching westwards to the Lake District and northwards to Tees-side. In addition, they were deeply involved in working iron, mining lead, quarrying stone, cattle rearing, horse breeding, and other industrial and agricultural concerns. Financial mismanagement, made worse by a series of unexpected catastrophes, brought economic collapse in the fourteenth century, but the monks recovered to be once again a flourishing concern with a vast fortune before the life of the abbey was brought to an abrupt end by the Dissolution of Henry VIII.

Cross the River Skell by the little thirteenth century bridge for the main approach to the abbey from the west, as it was in medieval times. The west front was built about 1160 from sandstone hewn from the rocky outcrops on the north side of the valley, and on entry you are greeted with an uninterrupted vista framed by the massive pillars.

Forward on your right is the south transept which marks the site of the first wooden church built in 1133 and the oldest part of the abbey. Imagine the scene as the monks filed down the night stairs from the adjoining dormitory and through this transept to enter the choir for night services which began with Matins about 2.00 am. On an arch you will see a carving of an angel holding three horseshoes (see box — page 74).

Gaze up at the great 172 foot high Perpendicular tower built from local limestone by Abbot Marmaduke Huby whose initials are alongside the inscription 'To the only God be honour and glory for ever'.

The nerve centre of monastic life was the cloister, the quadrangle protected on each side by covered arcades which communicated with every part of the great abbey. The scale of this must have been envisaged soon after the settlement was established here for the corners were set out as early as 1140.

Here the monks devoted themselves to prayer and meditation; here were kept books and a wax tablet on which the weekly duties of the monks were written; here was the chapter house, so-called because a chapter of the Rule of St Benedict was read at the daily meeting; and here was the warming room where wood fires burned from November until Easter.

The Refectory, Guest Houses, Infirmary, Chapel of Nine Altars and

Lucky Horseshoes

Horseshoes seem to have earned their lucky tag due to a combination of things: the fact that they were made of iron, which was credited with the power of driving away witches and evil spirits; and their association with horses, which were worshipped by the ancient Greeks. Though a horseshoe is made in the form of a C, symbolising Christ, it was held in awe long before that and was probably seen as a representation of the heavens.

A Christian — like the angel in the carving — is supposed to hang it convex side uppermost forming an arch to represent the sky, but a pagan hangs it points uppermost to prevent the luck running out.

Horseshoes were a way of protecting a house from bad luck and were used in early rites which were performed when the foundations were laid and when the first entry into a new house was made.

It is supposed to be very lucky to find a horseshoe. If you do, you should pick it up, make a wish, throw it over your shoulder and walk on without looking back at it. However, most people would take it home to hang over their door because its presence is believed to avert evil and bring good fortune.

Sailors, including Nelson, nailed horseshoes to the masts of their ships to avert storms and shipwreck.

Horseshoes may well have been given special powers by early man who wondered how the shoe could be fitted to the horse without pain.

A neat piece of horse-shoeing is the chief claim to fame of St Eloi who is described as being "tall, with a fresh complexion, his hair and his beard curling, his face full of angelic kindness and its expression grave and unaffected".

According to legend a horse possessed of the Devil was brought to him at his forge. Frisky beyond belief, the horse would just not stand still at his forge. Without a moment of hesitation he cut off the leg that needed shoeing, nailed on the horseshoe, and then put the leg back on the stump, using the sign of the cross to make it unite quickly and heal effectively!

Another version of the legend has it that he cut off all four legs and restored them. When a bystander tried to imitate him the result was a dead horse, whereupon St Eloi chided him and promptly restored the animal to life again.

Fountains Abbey. Another view of the central tower

many other parts of the great Cistercian ruin command attention, depending on how much time you have available before you take the path back down the valley on the left-hand side of the Skell. This was constructed by William Aislabie in the eighteenth century as a carriageway for the use of visitors to Studley royal.

William was also a member of Parliament but less ambitious and flamboyant than his father. However, he managed to succeed where his father had failed when, in 1768, he bought Fountains Abbey for £16,000 from the Messenger family. His father had tried as early as 1720 with an offer of £4,000 but had suddenly called off the deal — his neighbour then subsequently refused to sell.

In his landscaping of the approach to the abbey William also broke away from the formality of his father's garden and created an informal sweep of grass along the Skell with woods on the valley sides providing a natural frame to the east end on the monastic church. This disappears behind you as you skirt the Rustic Bridge and follow the path back to the canal gates where you entered.

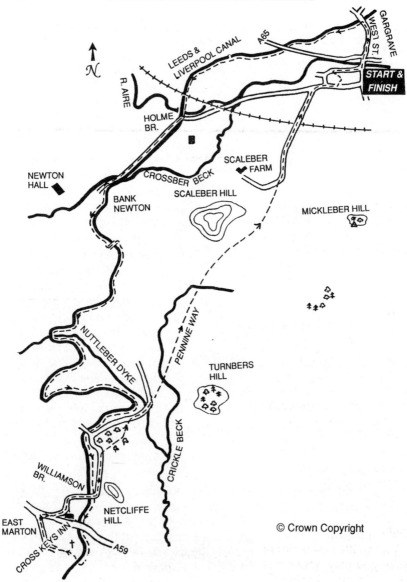

Pennine Panoramas

GARGRAVE

Approx. 8 miles

GARGRAVE, astride the A65 north of Skipton, was once a little inland port on the Leeds-Liverpool Canal linked by a specially built turnpike to the Duke of Devonshire's lead mines in Grassington. But it is the tranquillity of the canal and the panoramic views from its towpath that provides the attraction for walkers.

Starting from the centre of the village — where there is ample parking space — the canal towpath is reached by going up West Street and turning left. Although the towpath is not a right of way, British Waterways Board have raised no objection to well behaved walkers using the path.

Passing the first series of locks you may notice cast iron milestones indicating the distance between Leeds and Liverpool. Curving under the old Keighley-Kendal turnpike — now

Milestone along the Leeds & Liverpool Canal

the A65 — and the former London Midland & Scottish Railway, the canal crosses the River Aire at Holme Bridge. This fine aqueduct marked the terminus of the canal for a quarter of a century until enough finance was raised to continue construction work.

When the towpath twists out into a lane take the gate back on to the towpath to pass the spectacular series of locks at Bank Newton. When you reach the next bridge cross to the lane and enter the towpath on the left hand side to traverse an extremely beautiful section through open country. An enormous double curve demonstrates how the eighteenth century engineers followed the contour to avoid the expense

Double arch bridge over the canal at East Marton

of difficult embankments and locks — despite the increase in distance. Soon you enter a delightful wooded gorge with one of the cast iron mileposts near the unique double-arch bridge which carries the A59 from Skipton into East Lancashire. These arches are not arranged horizontally but vertically!

After a few hundred yards cross at the next bridge to East Marton church and enter the churchyard through a green gate. Continue up the lane to the main road and turn right to the *Cross Keys Inn*. Behind the inn is Bank Newton Lane which takes you back over the canal by Williamson Bridge and through a wood, turning right opposite a small tip to join the Pennine Way.

Follow the signs and path which leads over the pasture to an enclosed way which drops down to a stile. Above the gate ahead is a stile back into the lane. Continue right to the next Pennine Way sign and leave the lane by a bend at a gate and stile. Follow the sign to descend to a footbridge and stiles over Crickle Beck before bearing left along a shallow valley through a series of stiles.

Past a narrow copse on your left keep forward through a field gate and continuing in the general north-easterly direction climb a low summit with Scaleber Hill to the left and Mickleber Hill, with its white

Gargrave in the Sixteenth Century

William Camden came this way and in his *Britannia* of 1590 wrote:

"This Are springing out of the hill Pennigent, which among the Western hils mounteth aloft above the rest, doth forthwith so sport himself with winding in and out, and doubtful whether he should returne backe to his spring-head, or runne on still to the sea, that myselfe in going directly forward on my way was faine to pass over it seven times in an houres riding. It is so calme, and milde, and carryeth so gentle ans slow a streame, that it seemeth not to runne at all but to stand still, whence I suppose it tooke the name. For, as I have said before, Are in the British tongue betokeneth Milde, Still and Slowe; whereupon that slow River in France Araris hath his name.

The Country lying about the head of this River, is called in our tongue Craven, perchance of the British word Crage, that is, a Stone. For, the whole Tract there, is rough all over and unpleasant to see to, with craggy stones, hanging rocks and rugged waies; in the middst whereof, as it were in a lurking hole, not farre from Are standeth Skipton; and lyeth hidden and enclosed among steep Hilles, in the like manner as Latium in Italie, which Varro supposeth to have been called, because it lyeth close under the Apennine and the Alps. The Towne (for the manner of their building among these Hilles) is faire enough, and hath a very proper and strong Castle, which Robert de Rumely built, by whose posterity it came by inheritance to the Earles of Aumerle. And when their inheritance for default of heires fell by escheat into the King's hands, Robert de Clifford, whose heires are now Earles of Cumberland, by way of exchange obtained of King Edward the Second both this Castle, and also faire lands round about it every way, delivering into the King's hand in lieu of the same, the possessions that he had in the Marches of Wales."

trig point, on the right. Keep straight ahead to the left of a wooden fence towards a field gate, ignoring the temptation to follow the wall away to the right. The path from the left is joined by the track from Scaleber Farm and continues downhill across the railway from which the Pennine Way bears right, but the easiest way back to Gargrave is to continue until the track meets a lane.

Turn right here and take a path to the left through a black field-gate at the first pasture on your left. This leads down to the sparkling infant River Aire and with its stepping stones alongside the village green.

Way of the Waterfalls

INGLETON

Approx. 6 miles

WITH ITS NUMEROUS WATERFALLS, wooded gorges, limestone grasslands, interesting geological features, and spectacular open views there can be few, if any, more magnificent walks than this in the whole country. The modest entrance fee that you have to pay to enjoy them is therefore certainly good value for money. The location is Ingleton, reached on the A65 from Skipton and on the B6255 from Hawes in Wensleydale.

The entrance to the "Waterfalls Walk" is in the valley bottom and is dominated by a towering railway viaduct. Together with the Broadwood car park it is clearly signposted in the village.

Follow the walkway up the valley of the River Twiss which comes rushing down from Kingsdale as you proceed through the green, wooded valley. After passing through Creeping Steads — so-named because people had to creep before the well-defined path was made — the valley becomes a canyon between nearly vertical cliffs rising over two hundred feet as you enter Swilla Glen. Here there is an abundance of plant life amongst the hazel, ash, and oak trees that have weathered decades of wind and rain.

A footbridge called Manor Bridge takes you across the river which has scoured its way through the North Craven Fault which caused the upthrust and displacement of the rocks hereabouts. Evidence of the primeval uplift in the limestone with older slates and sandstones is clearly visible as you enter Pecca Glen.

Pecca Bridge is the second footbridge you encounter to cross the river again, and from it there is a fine view of the first section of Pecca Falls. The footpath passes close to the these falls and Hollybush Spout too. Awe-inspiring sights are the reward for the breathtaking effort of negotiating some two hundred steps in this part of the walk, but on

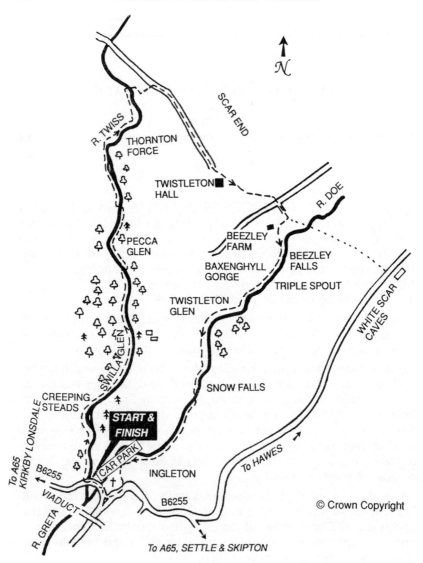

© Crown Copyright

climbing this steep hill there is a small refreshment bar where both sustenance and an opportunity for a welcome rest can be taken.

The route now continues along a much flatter section of the valley before passing Cuckoo Island to arrive at the spectacular Thornton Force waterfall. The waters of the River Twiss tumble fifty feet over the limestone rocks creating a crescendo of noise which accompanies you in the climb up the side of the fall.

Ahead are panoramic views across the limestone scenery to Spion Kop and Hunts Cross as you pass through the valley known as Raven Ray to cross a footbridge which marks the watershed from the valley of the River Twiss to that of the River Doe which flows down from Chapel-le-Dale. To reach it you traverse one of the ancient green roads which have served the sheep farmers here for thousands of years. Looking to the right there are good views of Bowland Knott, the outline of the Trough, and even into Quernmore.

Turn right along the green lane to pass Scar End and Twistleton Hall Farm which once served as a nunnery, before you drop down to cross the minor road from Chapel-le-Dale. Past Beezley Farm are stepping stones across the River Doe for anyone attracted by White Scar Caves across the valley in the shadow of Ingleborough. Otherwise bear right to follow the path alongside the River Doe for some more spectacular waterfalls.

First comes Beezley Falls to be followed by Triple Spout and the entrancing Baxenghyll Gorge where the more adventurous will opt for the view from the observation bridge high above the churning waters. The path continues past Snow Falls and with the descent comes a widening of the valley.

After crossing the river, relics of slate workings, limestone quarrying and abandoned lime kilns are mute reminders of former industrial glories. Soon the path joins the Hawes road where you bear right towards the railway viaduct to return to the car park.

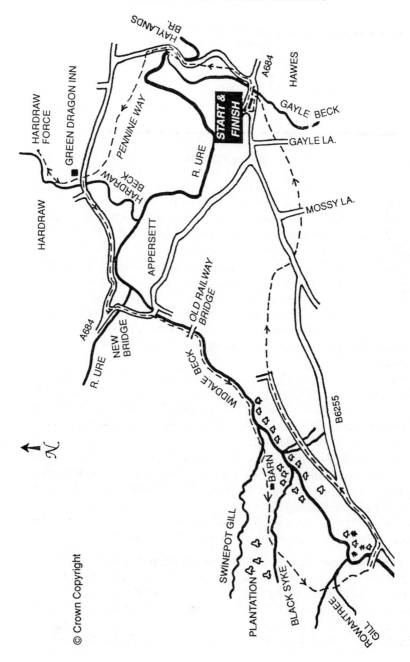

© Crown Copyright

By The Big Drop

HAWES

Approx. 10 miles

HAWES, CAPITAL AND OUTPOST OF UPPER WENSLEYDALE, lies on the A684 between Leyburn and Sedburgh. It is a rugged, straggling, thrown-about place, built of stone and bisected by the tumbling River Ure. Before the coming of the railway it was said to be one of the most inaccessible places in the country. Because of the difficult terrain hereabouts the pack horse lingered long after it had disappeared elsewhere and the railway came . . . and went.

Park in the town, then leave in the steps of the Pennine Way by heading north along Brunt Acres Road. Beyond the old railway bridge turn left along the paved footpath which traverses the field and returns to Brunt Acres Road which is carried over the River Ure by Haylands Bridge. Turn left up the steps shortly after the river bridge and follow the signposted path which runs through the fields to Hardraw where you can admire the spectacle of Hardraw Force — England's highest waterfall.

You enter the village alongside Hardraw Beck, and opposite is the *Green Dragon Inn* which provides access to the waterfall. From the public house go along the path on the right of the beck. It is possible with care to traverse in safety behind the fall and return down the opposite side of the stream — but it is probably best to retrace your steps back to the public house.

No better description can be coined than that of Arthur Norway who many years ago in *Highways & Byways of Yorkshire* wrote:

"The little stream brawls down the wood, gathering volume as its channel drops, and casting off its pretty wilfulness more and more, till at last it collects itself into one smooth, gleaming shot, and leaps down six and ninety feet into a black pool below. There is something in the aspect of this great cliff, this sudden stair breaking the monotony of the steady slope from the highlands to the level of the Ure, which is singularly striking and impressive. Conceive a precipice of lofty, blackened stone, curving round in a wide amphitheatre, absolutely sheer; and at its midpoint a slender stream shooting out into mid air, far away from the face of the cliff, a tangled column of fretted spray, broken at first into the semblance of filigree Venetian glass, intricate and silvery, but disintegrating as it falls, till at last it scatters into nothing more than a cloud of spray blown into the black pool, which lies waiting for it among large boulders at the foot of the descent. This is Hardaw Force and its beauty lies at the mercy of time."

With the *Green Dragon* on your right cross the bridge over Hardraw Beck and follow the lane. Soon it is joined by the River Ure on the left. At the next junction turn left to Appersett.

New Bridge carries the lane over the River Ure and just before the bridge over Widdale Beck a stile in the wall just past a bridleway sign on the right marks the path which you follow alongside the beck.

Stone walls cover the hillsides with a net of very large mesh and they look particularly striking when lightly covered with snow. But these walls disappeared after a remarkable snowstorm in January 1895 which blocked all roads between Wensleydale and Swaledale until nearly the middle of March. Routes were carved out leaving walls of snow 10 to 15 feet in height but the wind and fresh falls almost obliterated them as fast as they were cut. Dalesfolk in farms and cottages were faced with starvation and they resorted to building sledges in an attempt to break out of the icy grip and find food.

After about ¾ mile you reach Swinepot Gill which enters the beck from the right. Cross over, then follow the Gill's left bank up and out of the valley, turning left at the top of the hill towards a solitary barn. Continue through the gate by the barn, right through the next gate and head towards the plantation in the distance. Shortly before reaching it, turn left ninety degrees to cross Black Sike and follow a poorly defined route until reaching the tight gulley of Rowantree Gill. Go over the wall, right down the hill towards the footbridge and then up the track to the Hawes-Ingleton road B6255 and left again.

Where the road forks, bear left down the narrow lane for about half a mile. Where it turns left sharply, pass through the gate in front onto a path which brings you back to the Hawes-Ingleton road which you cross. From here into Hawes the route is well defined as it crosses first Mossy Lane and then Gayle Lane.

Winter in Hawes

Livestock auctions are still a major attraction for farmers from many miles around Hawes, and at the verge of living memory are the days when stock was stood or penned in the main street of the town. Farmers were "bow-legged wi' brass" because they carried gold coins to buy whichever animals took their fancy. Locals claim that on a busy Tuesday there have been wagons from every English county parked at Hawes auction mart. In 1982 the auctioneers talked their way through the sale of 159,000 sheep, 7,379 cattle and 7,555 calves.

In the winters of 1739 and 1880 Hardraw Force was frozen from top to bottom, making a hollow tube of ice. Any such unusual occurrence in those days was generally made the opportunity for a concert. And it was music that enhanced the fame of Hardraw because the sheltered ravine was found to have remarkable acoustic properties. So in 1885 several gentlemen in Hawes organised a band contest there. This was so successful that it became an annual event. Famous bands like Besses o' th' Barn, Black Dyke, White Temperance and others won some of their first prizes and are said to have made their names at these contests which thousands of people attended. Later, competitions for choirs were added. On one occasion a lady in a pale grey dress fell in the stream when trying to cross by the stepping stones. Her choir was the next to compete, so there was no time to get dry, and as she stood singing the water dropped in little pools all round her. Her choir won!

One year, as an extra attraction, Blondin, the tight-rope walker crossed the ravine on a rope and cooked an omelette in the middle, thus adding importance to the whole affair. But when band contests were started in London interest in those at Hardraw waned and the prizes proved unattractive to major bands.

Access problems were another factor which caused the annual fixture to falter, and in 1984 what was generally assumed would be the last competition was held.

But new landlords at the *Green Dragon* gave a sympathetic ear to the Yorkshire and Humberside Brass Band Association when they suggested a revival of the contest. As a result, in September 1989 the romantic setting once again echoed to the sound of brass as an open air battle was waged between rival bands in cut-throat competition before an audience which included numerous chain-bedecked mayors from local councils.

Some twenty bands from Cleveland, Durham, Lancashire and Yorkshire competed for eleven prizes, but more particularly to reinvigorate this unique competition on the road to former glory.

Treated to this musical extravaganza the spectators left in a somewhat different frame of mind from William and Dorothy Wordsworth who visited Hardraw in 1799. The poet, after walking behind the rushing waters, described their conception of what it must be like to be in such a retreat on a summer day. He wrote:

"We could not help feeding upon the pleasure which this cave, in the heat of a July noon, would spread through a frame exquisitely sensible. That huge rock on the right, the bank winding round on the left with its living foliage, and the breeze stealing up the valley and bedewing the cavern with the sweetest imaginable spray, and then the murmur of the water, the quiet, the seclusion."

Legend has it that at the beginning of the reign of Henry VIII the monks of Jervaulx had a small chantry at Hardraw, and the brethren who were in charge of it lived in Fossdale. Apparently one Thirler, a hanger-on who lived in the hall at Hardraw, and Eric, a farmer, had killed a man named Master Jostrel who lived near the edge of the scar, and buried him on the moor. As Jostrel was missing, the monks decided that he had killed himself and sent for a brother from Jervaulx to settle the matter. One stormy night Eric, to his horror, found the body of Jostrel at the bottom of Hardraw Scar; they had buried it too near the beck and it had been washed out in a flood. This discovery only seemed to confirm the monks' decision and they commanded that the body should be buried at the cross-roads on the moor with a stake through it. One night, three years later, Eric came to the hall and forced Thirler to go with him to do penance on Jostrel's grave, as he himself had done every year. At daybreak a drover and boy, bringing black cattle across the moor to a fair, found them clutched together on the grave. Thirler was dead, his face and right hand burnt, and his knife melted from the haft. Eric was burnt also, but was still breathing, and lived long enough to say that they were struggling with their knives when a thunderbolt had struck them.

By the author of *Waterside Walks in North Yorkshire*

Beyond the Bars
Ten Walks from York City Walls
by Ivan E Broadhead

The City of York is one of Britain's premier tourist centres and is justly famed for the multitude of historical features that make each visit such a memorable experience.

Many visitors, however, remain within the city walls, unaware that there is much more to explore and savour in the surrounding areas.

In this unique guide Ivan Broadhead presents ten walks starting at the ten traditional exits ("Bars") from the city walls and extending into the surrounding town, villages and countryside. The walks contain a wealth of historical and descriptive detail and feature rivers and streams, parks, monuments, churches and historic houses, and much else to captivate the attention of the reader.

"Each walk is a grand history tour: not a building, not a street with any semblance of a claim to fame is missed out. A fascinating mix of fact and legend." *Yorkshire Evening Post*

ISBN 1 869922 05 0. 190 pages, 10 maps, 84 photographs. £5.95

Available from booksellers or, in case of difficulty, direct from the publishers. Please send remittance plus £1.00 for postage and packing.

Meridian Books
40 Hadzor Road, Oldbury, Warley, West Midlands B68 9LA
Tel: 021-429 4397

An ideal walking companion

Let's Walk
by Mark Linley

Written for those who wish to join the increasing numbers who regularly escape the stresses and strains of modern life by walking in the countryside, in the hills and on the mountains, *Let's Walk*, in its sixteen chapters, gives advice and information on clothing and equipment, where to go, walking holidays, map and compass reading, wildlife, difficulties and hazards, first aid, weather, and much else.

The author, as well as being an experienced rambler, is also a skilled artist and the book is lavishly illustrated with cartoons which give a lively view of the walking scene.

"A splendid introduction to rambling. Give it to your children, in-laws, colleagues, neighbours. Or enjoy the wealth of information and 100 cartoons/sketches yourself." *The Rambler*

ISBN 1 869922 03 4. 144 pages. £4.95

Available from booksellers or, in case of difficulty, direct from the publishers. Please send remittance plus £1.00 for postage and packing.
Meridian Books
40 Hadzor Road, Oldbury, Warley, West Midlands B68 9LA